KU-114-166

JUNGLE TALES

MAINSTREAM / SPORT

JUNGLE TALES

CELTIC MEMORIES OF AN EPIC STAND

JOHN QUINN

MAINSTREAM
PUBLISHING

EDINBURGH AND LONDON

Copyright © John Quinn, 1994
All rights reserved
The moral right of the author has been asserted

First published in Great Britain in 1994 by
MAINSTREAM PUBLISHING COMPANY (EDINBURGH) LTD
7 Albany Street
Edinburgh EH1 3UG

This edition 1998

ISBN 1 84018 094 3

No part of this book may be reproduced or transmitted in any form or by any means
without permission in writing from the publisher, except by a reviewer who wishes to
quote brief passages in connection with a review written for insertion in a magazine,
newspaper or broadcast
A catalogue record for this book is available from the British Library

Typeset in Palatino
Printed and bound in Finland by WSOY

FOR my wife, Kathleen, and daughters, Julie, Karen and Joanna, for putting up with my long absences during research and writing. And to my sister-in-law, Julie, for her secretarial skills, which made what could have been a wearisome marathon typing exercise into a joyful sprint.

CONTENTS

ACKNOWLEDGEMENTS

My grateful thanks go to the very many people without whose assistance this book would not have been possible.

Special gratitude must be recorded to Bertie Auld, Pat Bonner, Liam Brady, Tommy Bums, Tommy Connolly, Kenny Dalglish, Terry Dick, Sean Fallon, Joe Gallagher, Peter Grant, Tom Grant, Davie Hay, Willie Haughey, Tom Lucas, Jimmy Johnstone, Jim McGinley, Jack McGinn, Matt McGlone, Billy McNeill, Paul McStay, Jimmy McVey, Lou Macari, Neil Mochan, Bob Ramsey, Arthur Reilly, Tony Roper, Jimmy Ruth and Pat Woods.

I am also indebted to many others from supporters clubs and individual fans – many of whom wrote to me without including an address.

To them and to everyone who helped in any way, I send my deep gratitude.

FOREWORD

I AM delighted to take this opportunity to pay tribute to the fans who occupied the Jungle during my time as a player and manager with Celtic.

There is no doubt in my mind that standing areas in football grounds have always been the focal point for the hard-core supporters of any team. Inevitably, it has been from the terraces that the real depth of feeling and emotion emanate and that is certainly the case with Celtic fans and the Jungle.

The supporters who congregated in that world-renowned area were always the first to appear at the game and invariably the last to leave.

There is no doubt in my mind that the Jungle made a major contribution to success at Celtic Park before, during and after my days there. The volume of support and the understanding and knowledge shown by the fans there is legendary. They were also the most colourful fans and, when in full flight, the Jungle was the most picturesque area of the ground, with the whole place a sea of green and white.

I have very many happy memories of my days with Celtic but two in particular will stick with me forever – the incredible noise from the fans and the astonishing sight of the Jungle on a big European night. I will never, ever, forget them and I thank the fans for providing me with those marvellous memories.

Billy McNeill

INTRODUCTION

IT does not seem too long ago to the days when the Jungle at
Parkhead, the Kop at Liverpool and Manchester United's Stretford
End were indisputably the best-known football terraces in Britain.
Indeed, their exalted place in the folklore of football would guarantee them high ranking among the best-known and most-beloved of
their type throughout Europe. Sadly all three have fallen victims to
the Taylor Report, which demands all-seated arenas in the interests
of safety.

But the fans who made these areas famous at Celtic, Liverpool
and Manchester United's grounds are not laughing at their passing.
And neither are the stars who paraded their skills before the massed
ranks of their adoring supporters. I have spent months researching
the feelings of the fans and players past and present, the men whose
names are a byword in sport, at the passing of their beloved terrace.
Players and fans alike tell tales of great excitement, depressing
sadness, humorous incidents and controversial happenings. All are
related with the enthusiasm of people who were as familiar with the
old north-enclosure terracing as they were with the comfortable
environs of their own living-room. It is an exercise in pure nostalgia,
a tribute to an era whose passing many fans will mourn.

Many of these stories are told by ordinary people whose lives
revolved around watching their idols in the green-and-white hoops.
Others are personalities from the world of showbiz who just loved
turning back the clock to the days of their youth, when they, too,
were simply fans who paid their cash to support *their* team. All of
them have one common interest – a love for a club that courses
through their veins regardless of performances on the field.

Some can recall the glory days of the marvellous Empire
Exhibition trophy-winning team of 1938, perhaps not as

eye-witnesses but having heard them lovingly recalled by their parents or grandparents. For many, the highlight of their very being is the marvellous night in Lisbon on 25 May 1967 when Celtic made glorious history in great banner headlines. On that occasion Jock Stein masterminded and Billy McNeill led Celtic to the unsurpassed achievement of becoming the first ever British team to taste glory at the highest level by winning the European Cup.

Fans from eight to 80 have stories to tell, spanning many generations, weaving a glorious history of a club currently undergoing hard times but those fans will never give up their hopes of a return to the top. One thing they can't do, however, is stand again on the small but so familiar terraces of the Jungle. But they have their memories to live on and they have enriched the tapestry of Glasgow Celtic FC.

Author's Note on Method and Organisation

IT all started when a sub-editor colleague on the *Evening Times* told me he thought there must be a book in the memories of the countless thousands of fans who had made standing in the Jungle to support their beloved Celtic a way of life.

But on researching the background to it and speaking to a wide variety of fans, I soon discovered it went deeper than that. To many, their sojourn on the terracings was almost a reason for existence. Their trips, on Saturdays and to midweek matches, took on almost pilgrimage proportions as they met up with fellow enthusiasts and exchanged stories.

To find out who they were and why their lives revolved around the gentle slopes of the old Jungle, I travelled many miles to interview fans and spent even longer on the phone and in reading letters that came from as far away as Australia. These letters and calls had come in response to articles in the *Evening Times*, the *Celtic View* and the fanzine *Once a Tim*.

In addition, I spent some great times chatting to such Jungle heroes as Jimmy Johnstone, Bertie Auld, Billy McNeill, Tommy Burns and many more, hearing their very personal recollections. Their stories and those of the fans were an education to me. I hope you enjoy them, too. They are presented in no special order and with no design on continuity. Each is an individual point of view but collectively they recall the special fascination that standing on the old terracings held for Celtic fans.

CHAPTER ONE

How 20,000 Celtic Fans Blew Away the Blues in the Jungle's Last Stand

JIMMY JOHNSTONE was in familiar territory, surrounded by friends whose company he treasured, but the wee man, whose unique football skills had made him a living legend, was becoming increasingly nervous with every passing minute. It had been some time since he had paraded his talents before the fans whose appreciation was his lifeblood, the supporters whose applause was, at one stage in his life, his main reason for living. He would die before letting them down and he knew this was his last chance to turn on a show for them in the only place that mattered both to them and to him. It was the final curtain on a career that had seen Johnstone soar to heights rarely ever achieved by a Scottish footballer. And sadly for the fans it was to be the last act on a stage that had been theirs for as long as even the oldest among them could remember.

We are talking about the end of an era, the closing chapter on a place where generations of Celtic fans had stood to cheer on their heroes. It was truly 'the Jungle's Last Stand'.

And wee Jimmy, who loved the fans who occupied that particular place, was being given his chance to play a part in letting the old area bow out in a style befitting its existence and history. But he wanted to make sure he did it right. He had to be on song with no mistakes. The skill that had been his hallmark throughout his illustrious career must not let him down. That was the reason for his nerves. That was why the butterflies were having a ball in the pit of his stomach. But the wee man was able to rise above it all and grown men wept unashamedly as he went through his extensive repertoire, for they knew after that it was to be all over.

Jimmy recalled his preparations for that night. 'We were all ready to give it everything we had,' said Jimmy. 'It was a great reunion night for the Lisbon Lions and we were taking on the Manchester United team that followed us in winning the European Cup a year after we had shown them all the way. But as I sat in the dressing-room with big Billy McNeill, Bobby Lennox and Bobby Murdoch, I was worried I wouldn't be able to play to my best and nothing less than that was going to satisfy me on this special occasion. Billy, Murdie and Lemon knew I was upset and did their best to calm me down. But I was going through torture. What made it worse was that a steward kept coming in to tell us how the crowd was growing. First he said there was about 5,000 fans there, which was fantastic considering the horrible weather all day. Then he said it had doubled and I thought, "That shows you just what special people these Celtic supporters are." But, honest to God, I nearly fainted when I heard there were almost 20,000 fans there at kick-off. I remember crossing myself and saying, "Please God, let me have a good game."' He added, 'For a minute I had forgotten it was not the real thing. It was not a big night in Europe. But when I think back now it was every bit as important, for it was something special for the fans to remember.'

Needless to say, Jinky Johnstone's fears were groundless. He was magical that night – as he had been for most of his career with Celtic – and the fans loved him all the more for it.

It had rained that night of 1 June 1993. No, that's not strictly accurate: it lashed down that night, as it had all day. But it would have taken more than mere water, no matter how many millions of gallons were to fall, to wash away the enthusiasm of the Parkhead fans on this night of nights. Earlier the fans, many of them in fancy dress, had rolled up in their thousands to mark the last official matchday, when Celtic beat Dundee 2–0 with goals by captain Paul McStay and Frank McAvennie. For fans whose minds are stacked with Celtic statistics, here is the team for that last official club match before the workmen moved in to demolish the old terracing:

Marshall, Smith, Boyd, Fulton, Wdowczyk, Galloway, Slater, McStay, McAvennie, Creaney, Collins. Substitutes: Grant and Miller.

A total of 16,000 certificates marking the occasion were printed by the *Evening Times* on this gala day and were handed out to the fans to become souvenirs of another era. All were eagerly accepted and such was the interest that the newspaper's office was bombarded for weeks by supporters desperate to get their hands on the special limited-edition keepsakes.

Although this was the final official *Celtic* match to be played there before the desecration of the terracing and the installation of the seats, it was not the last game witnessed from the Jungle. Ironically, that honour passed to Rangers fans as the light-blue army took over for the Scottish Cup final with Aberdeen, which ended with Walter Smith's men winning 2–1 to complete the domestic treble for the first time in 15 years.

It was for this reason the Parkhead directors decided to 'do a Sinatra' and have one last farewell appearance. 'Blow away the Blues' was how it was colourfully called and the Celtic fans rallied in true style.

Andrew Smith, now editor of the club newspaper the *Celtic View*, and then a reporter, summed it up perfectly, saying, 'For 19,316 fans to turn up at Celtic Park in absolutely dreadful weather for what was basically a couple of charity matches and a sing-song is nothing short of astonishing. It was yet another remarkable demonstration of the depth of feeling that Celtic supporters have for their club and proof that such passion and commitment remains as powerful as ever, despite recent years without success. It was an evening to say farewell to the Jungle as a standing area and pay one last tribute to the Lisbon Lions at the end of their testimonial year. Fittingly, these two institutions which have become such an important part of the fabric of being a Celtic fan were given a superb send-off.'

What a night it was as stars of today and yesteryear mixed with fans and celebrities alike, all with a common aim to give the Lions and the Jungle a send-off never to be forgotten. They achieved their goal – and then some.

The Peatdiggers supplied the background music as the fans kicked off the evening with a five-a-side competition. Then that bunch of well-known football fanatics who masquerade under the name of Dukla Pumpherston (and who raise marvellous amounts of money for charity) faced a celebrity select.

The Dukla side included such well-known characters as actor and playwright Tony Roper, whose work with Jonathon Watson is Only an Excuse for having fun. He was accompanied by former world fly-weight boxing champion Pat Clinton and former players

Gerry Collins and John McCormack, both of whose lifelong regret is that they never played for Celtic. Those who had worn the hoops loved pulling on the jerseys again – they included Danny McGrain, Peter Latchford, Jackie McNamara, Roddie MacDonald, and Ally Hunter. Robert Russell, once of Rangers and Motherwell, was also in their ranks. The celebrities side included television stars Michael Le Vell (of *Coronation Street*) and Patrick Robinson (of *Casualty*). The result mattered not one bit, but for the record Dukla ran out 3–1 winners.

Then came the moment the near 20,000 crowd had waited for when Billy McNeill led out his Lions to take on the Red Devils who, of course, included former Celtic star Pat Crerand in their number. The Lions were all there, except Willie Wallace who was in Australia, and misty eyes were par for the course in the Jungle as the heroes took their bow. Pat Crerand was accompanied in the United side by Bill Foulkes, Nobby Stiles and David Sadler from the Cup-winning side. They were boosted by former Celts John Fallon, Jim Brogan, Tommy Callaghan, Roddie MacDonald and Jackie McNamara.

With respect to the others, it was Jinky's night. With his dressing-room nerves conquered, the wee man turned on the style in his inimitable fashion. He was more like an 18-year-old than 48 as he showed the Jungle fans what they have been missing in recent years. Always one for the main chance, he hammed it up for all he was worth and the fans responded with deafening applause. Joe Craig scored twice and Frank McGarvey got the other in a 3–1 win for the Celts, who also included Murdo MacLeod in their side, but again the result was immaterial – it was the occasion that won the day. Pat Crerand, who had worn both colours with distinction, loved every minute of it. He said, 'Fantastic is the only way to describe that night. It was unbelievable that so many fans turned out on a night like that to give the Jungle a send-off. I used to stand in there as a kid, right on the halfway line, and I felt like jumping over there again when wee Jinky was running amok during the game – but the old legs would never have got over the barriers. Another man who enjoyed it was Nobby Stiles, who has always been a Celtic man anyway. During a lap of honour I saw him nipping round the track nicking piles of Celtic scarves for his grandchildren.' Pat, who had switched strips during the game, said it had been a great feeling to pull on the old green and white strip for one more time.

Frank Worthington, one of England's all time great ball-players, said, 'It was the first time I had played at Celtic Park and what a night to be there. The fans were magnificent. The lads just couldn't believe it.'

Mick McCarthy, who had played for Billy McNeill for Celtic and Manchester City, said, 'Brilliant sums it up for me.' He added, 'What made it even better for me was that I was not supposed to be playing and walked about with a long face until someone got tired of me sulking and asked me to play.' Mick, who loved his brief spell as a Celtic player, added, 'I never expected such an atmosphere but remembering those magnificent fans I should have known better.'

Murdo MacLeod, whose name is included in the record books as one of Celtic's multi-award winners, said, 'To play in front of the Jungle again was pretty special and the atmosphere was electric.'

Former Celtic captain Andy Lynch said, 'Celtic fans are, without doubt, the finest fans in the world and they proved it that night. It was tremendous fun.' The stars of showbiz also had a ball. *Coronation Street*'s Bill Tarmey, whose name will forever be linked with a character called Jack Duckworth, was self-styled 'chief coach' of the celebrity team and later declared himself none too happy with the result. Laughingly, he recalled, 'Dukla's third goal was suspiciously offside and we were denied two stonewall penalties. Despite all that, though, it was a wonderful night.'

Greg Kane, one part of pop group Hue & Cry, admitted that, like Jimmy Johnstone, he had an attack of nerves beforehand. Despite countless big-occasion concerts with brother Pat, Greg said, 'It was nerve-wracking but tremendously enjoyable. I didn't know if we would be supplied with strips so I brought my own Celtic away top anyway. It was fantastic to help celebrate the final night of the Jungle and it was a very emotional night.'

Patrick Robinson, who plays Martin Ashford in *Casualty*, normally teams up with the *Coronation Street* lads for charity matches but said he had never seen anything like the Jungle's Last Stand. 'It was just incredible and a dream come true to play in front of such a large crowd. The fans were magnificent and really gave it everything.'

But the showbiz star who seemed to take more from the occasion than anyone else was Michael le Vell (*Coronation Street*). Michael said later he was absolutely thrilled as the Jungle fans chorused, 'There's only one Kevin Webster.' Sally's man from the Street joked, 'I knew who they meant!' He added, 'That really made my night. A tingle went down my spine when I realised what they were singing. It was one of the greatest moments of my life because we are used to playing before just a few hundred people.'

We Want the Parrot

IN my dozen or so years watching my football from the Jungle I have heard some amazing cries of encouragement, anger, frustration, and sheer delight – but the one to beat them all was surely: 'We want the parrot!' And unfortunately it referred to me. It all came about after my wife, Katrina, hit on the idea to hire a colourful parrot costume for me to take part in the fancy-dress carry-on as part of the Jungle's Last Stand. It went down a treat with the fans and took the hearts of the Jungle fans that great, but sad, day.

Unfortunately, I was too late to enter the competition but when the *Celtic View* appealed for the fan who had been wearing the costume to come forward, I got in touch to own up that it was me. The outcome was magnificent. My wife and I (that sounds like something out of my wedding speech) were guests of the club for a day. It was fabulous and I got my season ticket for the Jungle's first term as an all-seated area. But the credit for everything goes to Katrina. It was her idea from the start and it paid off in style. I must say, though, when she showed me the costume at first I wasn't too keen. Katrina pointed out it was just for fun so I decided to go for it, and I am glad I did. The fans in the Jungle were, as usual, fantastic, although I should have known that, having stood there among them for 12 years.

I must own up and say Celtic are my life. We got engaged at Parkhead and even got married on a Friday so that we could go back to the Jungle the next day. But, I digress. That day of the fancy-dress parade I didn't realise those taking part had to be there at a certain time and place so I thought I had lost out when I saw the people making their way to the tunnel. The fans were great though, for they had picked me out (you couldn't really have missed me in that lot) and started pushing me to the front. When I made my way on to the track I was stopped from going any further, but the Jungle kept on chanting, 'We want the Parrot.' It was a dream come true to stand there and hear the Jungle shouting for me, even though I knew it was the parrot and not me personally they were cheering. The fans kept up their shouts and I suppose it was really appropriate to say I was 'sick as a parrot' when I did not get to join in the competition as I was too late.

But it all ended when the *View* appealed for me to come forward and the day at Parkhead and the season ticket proved the ideal prescription for my parrot sickness. Although they have taken away my standing space, I am delighted to be still there as the Jungle is *the* only place to watch the football. Now I just sit there and roar on the boys, hopefully, to success next season.

Vincent Stevenson, Anderston

TO be honest, I am a Celtic End regular, but I couldn't miss out going to the Jungle today on its last official day of action. I had no idea I would be the first in but I am delighted. Getting this certificate has just made it all the more memorable for me.

Andrew Hillan (17) who queued for 90 minutes to get into the Jungle on its last day

IF Andrew Hillan was first to get into the Jungle on its last day, then 15-year-old Robbie Miller, from South Queensferry, also made history by being last admitted: 'I made a run for it and squeezed through before the gates closed. The certificate is a fabulous reminder and just capped a really brilliant day. I've been coming to the Jungle for three years but this day has been the best ever for me.'

I TOOK my son, Craig, along to see the Lisbon Lions taking their final bow in front of a standing Jungle. Jimmy Johnstone and Bobby Lennox were the great entertainers and the Jungle was the place to be entertained. It's been an exhilarating place to be for me in the last 25 years and I'll miss it.

Eddie Gillan, Maryhill

WE usually go to the stand, but we went to the Jungle for the last great occasion. It was my first time in there, and unfortunately my last, but I enjoyed it.

James Queen (9), Beattock, who went to 'the Jungle's Last Stand' with his cousin, Edward

THE Jungle's the place where the *real* people have stood but now I suppose we'll have to move to the Celtic End until they knock that down.

Thomas Kerr, Provanmill Celtic Supporters Club, (who won one of the ten best fancy-dress awards on the last day)

THE Jungle has been the place capable of lifting the team to great heights and I've watched some great footballers from this part of the ground. For me Charlie Tully was the most magical of them all. I feel it has quietened down over the past few seasons and has lost something. But it still has been a great area to have been to watch, every home match, to share in some great times over the years.

John Rainey (71)

I BROUGHT my cardboard cut-out of Paul McStay and Paul signed it before I took my place in the Jungle queue on that last day. I know Paul used to come to this part of the ground so it's right that the two of us should be here together on the Jungle's last afternoon.

Jim Wheland, Stirlingshire's Paul McStay No. 1 Supporters Bus

I'VE been going to the Jungle for about two seasons and the best atmosphere I can remember was the night we beat Cologne in the UEFA Cup. It was unbelievable.

James McKinstry (13), Govanhill

It's now ten years since I started going to the Jungle and I always felt very comfortable there, meeting my pals, Pat McLaughlin, Terry Reynolds and Michael Barry, at every home game.

Rachel Hobbs, Partick

First Visit to the Jungle at the Age of Eight

THE first time I was taken to the Jungle I was only eight years old and was far too wee to see what was happening, so I was pushed down to the front along with the other kids. I suppose, looking back on it, my view from the front row in the Jungle, right at the side of the running track, must have been akin to the World War I Tommy peering over the trench top into no-man's land. Anyway, all I can remember seeing was legs, some of them in white stockings. I'm told that Bobby Evans, Bobby Collins and Charlie Tully were playing then, as it was in the Fifties. But all I had was my father's word for that as I couldn't match faces to legs. Nowadays we watch the Italian football on the television and hear all about their 'technical area' at the front. It makes me laugh as we had that years ago in the front of the Jungle, but the technical experts were us kids.

That first look from the front put me off a wee bit, simply because I couldn't see the action. And I didn't go back there for about ten years. But one night I went there to see Celtic playing Rangers and it was the game when Kai Johannsen missed a penalty. Ronnie Simpson set Celtic off right away and they eventually ran out 3–1 winners over Rangers. That, for me, was a memorable night in season 1967–68 as Celtic beat Rangers in the League Cup. But it was also the night Richard Kimble, the 'Fugitive' on television, found the one-armed man he had been chasing and proved his innocence for all to see.

While I could never class myself a regular, I went to the Jungle often with my mates from Ruchazie No. 1 Supporters' Club, George Barr, Brian Docherty and others, as well as Jim Diamond, who went on to become a famous pop star – 'I Should Have Known Better', etc. We were all standing there one day when the ball was punted down the park and Bobby Lennox set off in chase. The wee Buzz Bomb was too fast for everyone and consequently was declared offside. The verdict was greeted by the usual Jungle jeers and as Bobby made his way back up the park Jim Diamond was still shouting and bawling. This time, though, the linesman must have been right for this gorilla shouted at Jim, 'Look son, we all know Lennox is fast, but he's no an effing greyhound.' Dido's face matched his hair – red!

Soon after that I went abroad and haven't been in the Jungle for 25 years. I had been looking forward to going back for old times' sake but now, with the seating installed, I have lost that chance so I have only my boyhood memories to live on.

W. Boyle, Ruchazie

MY friend, Andrea McFall, and I make the trip from Belfast half a dozen times a season and we've been doing that for about six years. We'll still make the 17-hour round trip but we'll really miss standing in the Jungle.

Susan Donnelly, Ardoyne

MY first experience of the Jungle was 23 years ago as a three-year-old when I scored a hat-trick playing with a tin can on the old terracing. The fact that my dad was watching me and the Celtic *v* Partick Thistle reserve game did not mean much to me at the time and apparently his remarks to my mother when we got home were all about 'never again'. But he obviously didn't mean it as I was back there with him on countless occasions and would never go anywhere else until they stuck a seat on my halfway-line spot.

Gary Scott, Liverpool

have made a fine job of this new area. The seats are grand and the view from here is quite superb. But it's not the Jungle, is it? Where's the excitement? Where's the camaraderie? Through the years fans used to build up a rapport with all their mates standing around them and also with the team. I believe if the powers-that-be are not careful they will turn football into something more like a night at the pictures. Football is all about fans. It's about people showing emotions, getting caught up in the passion of the game. I know I'll be challenged on this but you can't do that sitting down, politely applauding. I know we must have progress. I accept you must upgrade the stadia. I also accept you must have comfort. But in my view you can do that equally well standing as you can sitting, providing you conform to certain standards. By all means give supporters who want seats their own comfortable place where they can dine and wine and watch the game in circumstances they demand. And I realise the bulk of them will want to sit nowadays. That's all very well, and I am certainly not denying anyone that right. But equally I feel strongly that the Jungle area, or standing area, or whatever name you want to give it, should have a place within the modern stadia. There should be a special place set aside where fans can stand if that is what they want to do. Surely that is their right? If that's what they want then we should provide it for them; but with safety, with a roof, with all the facilities they require; there should be toilets for men and women, for there must be a place for female fans, too.

'Give them that place, make it as comfortable as you can with a café-complex and let them get on with it. We always used to admire the German stadia and I've been in a few in recent times. They are comfortable, they have seats to comply with safety standards. But they also have huge standing areas and they are the first to fill up on match days. All right, I know they are cheaper, but surely that tells you that the fans also want freedom of choice. That was denied them in this country when no one challenged the Taylor Report. And it went unchallenged because, at that time, it was a political bombshell coming so soon after the terrible disasters at Bradford and Hillsborough when so many people died. That was awful and I feel so bad about people dying in such terrible circumstances, but that is why this legislation went ahead without being challenged. However, it does not alter my view that people deserve the right to choose. That is the very essence of our democracy and I will never change my view that fans should be allowed to make up their own minds. We have become soft, and I know that I, too, have graduated to using the stand, but I know very many people who would, even in these great modern stadia, still like to exercise their right to choose and that has been denied them.'

It is now many years since Billy's Aunt Grace took him on the road from their home, in the four-in-a-block house in Bellshill, that was to lead to unparalleled fame as Celtic captain and manager. And Billy has many fond memories of those early days – especially the ones spent with that very special breed of men, 'The Lisbon Lions'. His one regret is that neighbour Dan Gallagher, who lived downstairs from the McNeills, and who ran the Celtic Supporters bus faithfully week-in week-out for years, died before seeing his young friend grow up to captain the team to fame in Lisbon. Billy recalls: 'Old Dan died just before Lisbon and that saddened me as he, more than anyone, deserved to have enjoyed that marvellous occasion as a reward for all his faithful service to the club.' Billy's 'début' as a fan came three years after the end of the Second World War when he first set foot on Parkhead soil in that old, dilapidated Jungle area. The country was slowly but surely getting back on its feet and football was returning to its peak. Celtic were not winning much, but they were still fine entertainers, including such stalwarts as Bobby Evans, John McPhail and Willie Miller. But a new star had arrived on the horizon – one Charles Patrick Tully, one of seven footballing brothers from Belfast, who was to carve his name on the Scottish football scene in letters tenement-high. Within weeks of his first appearance in 1948, Charlie was to earn the accolade 'The Clown Prince of Soccer', and no one deserved it more than the extrovert Charlie, who signed on from Belfast Celtic for the transfer fee of £8,000 – which some so-called stars earn on a weekly basis these days. Settling quickly, Charlie soon became the darling of the Jungle fans and the young McNeill, having heard all the talk in the school playground in Bellshill, Lanarkshire, wanted to see this man who had captured the imagination of the nation. Aunt Grace decided one day in August 1948 that the time had come and the lad who was to go on to become a living legend in Scottish football, the first Briton to hold aloft the coveted European Cup, was beside himself with joy. 'I'll never ever forget that day,' laughs Billy, 'not because of the football, although I thought Tully was terrific, but because Aunt Grace lost a heel on her shoe and I felt I was to blame for making her take me to the packed Jungle instead of the terracings, which were not quite so full. But to me that was the start of my love affair with that old area and when I look back on it now, I realise just how much we have lost with its closure.'

But if Tully was the first player Billy saw making the most of the wholesale backing of the Jungle he was certainly not to be the last. Billy mentions two 'Lions' in particular who just loved parading their special talents to the fans in the Jungle. The Jungle certainly had a much greater influence over some players than others but McNeill, who ought to know from years of experience, cites Jimmy Johnstone and Bertie Auld as the best examples of players being tuned into the Jungle fans: 'Jimmy loved nothing better than flying up and down the wing in front of the Jungle. And wee Bertie milked it to the fullest extent. Equally, the fans loved it as their heroes turned it on for their benefit. And I have to admit that, although John Clark and I were essentially central-area players, we also cashed in on the lift you undoubtedly got from the Jungle. John and I used to say to each other we wanted to drift over to the Jungle side early on in a game. If you could get in a decisive tackle or make a telling clearance in front of the fans there, you knew you were on to a good game.

'I have countless memories of great games played at Parkhead but one stands out from the rest. It was the return leg of our European Cup tie with the French club St Etienne. We were down 2–0 from the first leg and as time wore on in the first half at Parkhead we were showing no signs of breaking down their well-organised defence. Then, as half time approached, Bobby Murdoch took a throw-in way down at the Jungle end. Joe McBride was astute enough to burrow his way into the penalty box with some great twisting and turning and a French defender clattered him and Joe went down. The roar from the Jungle was ear-splitting and I'm not saying we wouldn't have got the penalty anyway, but it was one of those that could have gone either way and the roar from the Jungle certainly helped in our favour. Tommy Gemmell scored from the award and we went on to win 4–0, with Jim Craig, Steve Chalmers and Joe McBride getting the other goals. I have no doubt that was the turning point and that incredible roar from the Jungle proved the deciding factor.

'There were many more memorable occasions, but one I remember with great affection was in our centenary year when we won the Double and the Jungle serenaded the club with "Happy Birthday Dear Celtic". That, to me, summed up both their loyalty and their inventiveness. Mind you, I should not have been surprised, as it has always been the Jungle that has led the singing. I used to wonder where all the spontaneous singing originated. I mean, do they rehearse them on the bus on the way there? Whatever they do, they are brilliant at it. Big Jock used to say that the fans were worth a goal of a start and he was not far off the mark. I used to look on the Jungle as a barometer of how well we were doing. If it was packed we were assured of terrific backing. Equally, if it was quiet we knew we were going to struggle. Thankfully, it was rarely quiet as it was a very popular place to be and there was a life about it that made it unique. I used to watch Argentinian football on television and they had huge standing areas which were reminiscent of the Jungle. They had a bounce about them that made me think back to my playing days at Parkhead. I also enjoy watching German football as their stadia were once held in high esteem by British clubs. They were thought to be the leaders in design but when you look at them now you find they still have the big Kop area where fans love to stand. I recall speaking to the renowned Dutch coach Will Koerver, and he told me on many occasions that he loved coming to Parkhead simply to savour the atmosphere. He said we were fortunate to have that and this was a missing ingredient in his country.'

It is natural, I suppose, for McNeill to have a special feeling for European football as this special arena brought him so much recognition. And Billy is first to admit he enjoyed the big nights of the European challenge more than any other: 'There's nothing quite like it for fans and players alike. I felt it was the proper theatre for the game. The atmosphere is quite magnificent and we used to deliberately run out for a warm-up half an hour before kick-off at Parkhead. This had a dual purpose as it served to get the players in the mood and it also got the crowd going. Many a time we had to go back in to get a rub-down before going back out for the kick-off but we were so psyched up by the crowd we would have walked through brick walls. They had this tremendous ability to lift and inspire you and the players lived off it. I hope I am not being unfair to the supporters in other parts of the ground, in particular the Celtic End. They, too, were tremendous to us, but I always felt they waited to take their lead from the Jungle and then gave it full throttle. It was always my wish at Celtic that, when redevelopment was taking place, we should have brought the Celtic End nearer to the pitch. It was a great big super bank of fans but they were just too far away from the action, whereas the Jungle was right on top of the players. That's just a thought for the planners, but if I had my way that's what I would do and, if that was repeated at the other end, who knows, maybe you would then have the equivalent of a Jungle on all sides.'

BILLY MCNEILL is most certainly not alone in saying the authorities should have made provision for fans to be allotted a standing place in the new set-up for football grounds in the modern era. Indeed, he is in good company, for among those who share his beliefs and view-point, and is equally unafraid of saying so, is Kenny Dalglish – Scotland's most capped player, who represented Scotland on 102 occasions, scoring 30 goals.

And the man who was to follow McNeill as a Celtic great, before moving to enjoy even greater success with Liverpool, states quite frankly that the fans' thoughts should have been taken into consideration.

No one has done more for the cause of crowd safety than Kenny and no one has been more deeply affected by the tragedies which have marred the game. When at Anfield, he was a witness to the Heysel and Hillsborough disasters which claimed so many lives and left scars on the families affected by the terrible toll of death and injury. It was as a result of the Hillsborough disaster in 1989 that Lord Justice Taylor was commissioned to produce the report on crowd safety which went on to recommend all-seater stadia.

But while work was going on at his Ewood Park home of Blackburn Rovers, converting it to an all-seated ground, Kenny was giving his views to a BBC2 programme, *Standing Room Only*. Kenny told the television interviewer: 'All-seater stadia were brought in for all the right reasons, but I think there are a lot of people who would prefer to stand and watch matches. Clubs are spending a fortune and doing the grounds up for the benefit of the fans, but maybe they could have done that and still allowed them to stand at the same place.

'At Liverpool you would see the same people at the same spot, week in week out. They had their own spot allocated to them and were within a couple of feet of it at every home game. The same person would be stood at the same spot because there were so many season-ticket holders, so in itself it was a club within a club.

'I am no politician and I am not going to start beating any drums and say there should be any legislation against it. All I would say is that I think it takes a little bit from the supporters' choice of whether they can sit or stand at a game.'

IT is no secret that the fans in the Jungle were unhappy at having the seats installed and, if it is any consolation, they are not alone.

Supporters from a representative selection of clubs in England voiced their opinion on a BBC television programme called *Sit Down and Shut Up*. On this programme, fans from Liverpool, Manchester United and Arsenal in particular all told the same story of how they had wanted to be left alone to watch their football as they had always done – standing on their favourite part of the stadium. Rogan Taylor, a keen fan and football historian, said the game had changed from being the working man's sport to a big business and it had been spoiled in the process. Elderly Liverpool fan Billy O'Donnell was upset as he said the change meant he could no longer afford to follow his favourites. 'They don't have testimonials for fans,' was his mournful but accurate lament. His views were backed by a survey which showed that 92 per cent of Anfield fans preferred standing on the Kop to sitting down to watch. And even FA Chief Executive Graham Kelly admitted he rarely sat down to watch a game if it was possible to stand.

Open Space, BBC TV, 12 May 1993

United in Grief

30 APRIL 1989 was an emotional day in the history of two football clubs. It was a day when the supporters of Celtic and Liverpool joined forces and forged links between two clubs, two sets of fans and two cities in a powerful and public show of emotion in tribute to those who had died in a football tragedy.

The death of 95 Liverpool fans, whose lives had been cut short at their club's match at Hillsborough two weeks before, had left the nation stunned.

Kenny Dalglish, the Anfield manager, who had been a hero to the Celtic fans in his ten years at Parkhead, undoubtedly did the right thing in turning to his old club to supply the opposition for the Hillsborough Charity Appeal fund. It was a decision of which he was to be made immensely proud as more than 60,000 fans gathered to pay tribute to the dead in a unique and highly emotional occasion, the likes of which had never been seen at Parkhead before. In the end Liverpool won 4–0 but Kenny rightly declared the result irrelevant on a day when only the fund mattered.

Ten minutes after the final whistle Dalglish, who had defied the years to show glimpses of his incomparable form, was forced to return to the field as the fans delivered a magnificent rendition of their joint anthem 'You'll Never Walk Alone' with countless thousands of scarves, green, white and red, raised in a show of acclaim. It was an unforgettable sight on an unforgettable day.

A massive banner in green, white, red and blue proclaimed the message 'Merseyside Thanks Glasgow' and this bore fulsome testimony to what the day had been all about. Ninety-five scarves, knotted together in silent tribute to those who had died, were laid at the area where most of the Liverpool contingent of fans were gathered. Kenny said: 'That unbelievable reception was obviously a great benefit to my players. Just what it will have done to their minds after resuming playing is not yet clear. Everyone came here to pay their respects. They were all magnificent. I knew we would get a great reception but I did not believe it would be as good as that.'

Looking at the backdrop of the Jungle, awash in green and white and red, his captain, Alan Hansen, said: 'We needed that game and it was a tribute to Celtic that they played two days in a row for us.' The Liverpool chairman, John Smith, joined in the praise, saying: 'Celtic are a particularly warm club with great fans. This was tremendous and forges even closer the links between us.' His Parkhead counterpart at the time, Jack McGinn, said: 'We wanted to raise as much money as we could for the disaster fund and at the same time provide Liverpool with a platform to get back to playing football in a friendly and welcoming atmosphere. We have exceeded our expectations in both aims.'

Liverpool rediscovered the exhilaration of playing the people's game at Celtic Park in front of 60,437 people whose generosity of spirit manifested itself in an emotional, touching celebration of the brotherhood of fans.

HOWEVER unimportant the contest as a competitive exercise, and however poignant the circumstances, it takes a special breed of football supporter to dismiss a 4–0 defeat with an unstinted tribute to the opposition.

The scarves, mainly the green and white of Celtic but with a tinge of Liverpool red, hoisted around the stadium at the end as a backdrop to 'You'll Never Walk Alone', served to convey the empathy that exists between followers of football teams in time of tragedy.

Even more important, the Hillsborough Charity Appeal will

benefit to the extent of around £500,000 and, when that is considered the scoreline, as the hero of both cities Kenny Dalglish said, becomes 'irrelevant'.

Ian Paul, *The Herald*, Monday, 1 May 1989

GARY GILLESPIE, who was one of Liverpool's brightest stars and who was later to bring his unique style to Celtic Park, played for Liverpool that day and to this day has never forgotten the occasion.

Much later, writing in the Celtic View of 12 May 1993, Gary said: 'It was a fantastic afternoon, overwhelming. The fact that the game was a 61,000 sell-out at such short notice said everything about the depth of feeling Celtic supporters had over the events of Hillsborough. The generosity and warmth shown towards Liverpool made it an absolute pleasure to play that day. By Liverpool I don't just mean the football club. I feel that the fans, through their banners and chants, were demonstrating their affinity with the people of Liverpool and the city itself. By their actions they were saying, "Our sympathies go with you. We understand the pain felt by your city and we are united in that grief."

'It was a unique and highly emotional coming together of two clubs and showed that a real empathy existed between the two sets of fans. It created a quite incredible atmosphere to play in and gave an indication of the power supporters can have when they concentrate their efforts positively. The blur of the green-and-white scarves of Celtic mingling with the red-and-white ones of Liverpool all around the stadium and the joint choruses of "You'll Never Walk Alone" created unforgettable scenes.'

Gary added: 'There had been a lot of grieving and soul searching in the days and weeks following the tragedy and the players were unsure how it would affect us when we started playing again. But the way the whole stadium got behind us and willed us to get back to playing the kind of football we were producing that season helped settle us down.'

LIVERPOOL'S first game since Hillsborough, where 95 fans died, was always going to be significant in the hearts and minds of those who hold the club dear.

And the good Glasgow people made it a day to remember for all the right football reasons. Over 60,000 fans queued in orderly fashion

– many wearing the green of Celtic and the red of Liverpool – to raise an astonishing £500,000 for the Hillsborough Charity Appeal.

The 7,000 fans who made the 400-mile round trip from Liverpool mixed freely among the crowd. Here were people united in a common love of football and you could almost reach out and feel the warmth.

Liverpool players came out in ones and twos to a great reception in the warm-up, but that was nothing compared to the thunderous roar of applause as the teams came out to the haunting strains of 'You'll Never Walk Alone'.

Thousands of green Celtic scarves suddenly took the salute in one of the most remarkable messages of friendship I can ever remember at a football ground. The teams stood around the centre circle, Celtic and Liverpool players together, to observe the minute's silence. A banner on the touchline read 'Merseyside Thanks Glasgow' and the great amphitheatre became silent.

Kenny Dalglish, a player held in great respect both in Glasgow and Liverpool, appeared for 56 minutes and showed glimpses of the style that made him world class. The crowd cheered him to the rafters during and after the game. And at the end, he was persuaded away from the warmth of the dressing-rooms to take a salute as his name echoed round the ground.

But, as Kenny said at the finish, it was not a day about football, but about paying respect to those who died at Hillsborough.

Ken Gaunt, *Liverpool Echo*, 1 May 1989

TRADITIONALLY, this space in a football programme is given over to some words from the home team manager, but today we are using it for words about the Celtic team manager.

On the day of his first home game in charge of Celtic as manager for the second time, we would like to welcome Billy McNeill home to Celtic Park on behalf of the entire Celtic support.

As a player, team captain and manager he has been a great favourite of the support in the past and is sure to be a favourite again in the future.

This month will see the 29th anniversary of the day Billy met the Celtic support for the first time as a player when he made his début in the hoops for a League Cup match with Clyde at Celtic Park on 23 August 1958. Celtic won 2–0.

As every Celtic fan knows, Celtic won every tournament they entered in season 1966–67 and during that clean sweep Billy missed only one game, on 5 November 1966, when Tommy Gemmell took over the No. 5 shorts for a league meeting with St Mirren at Celtic Park. The game ended 1–1, with Gemmell scoring Celtic's goal. On 3 May 1975 McNeill played his last game for Celtic, his only senior club, and was on the winning side against Airdrie in the Scottish Cup final. Airdrie were on the receiving end of a 3–1 result.

In all, he played 776 games for Celtic, winning nine League Championship medals, seven Scottish Cup winner's medals, six League Cup winner's medals, one European Cup winner's medal and 29 Scotland caps. A collection second to none.

CELTIC PROGRAMME, challenge match *v* Arsenal, 1 August 1987

THE Liverpool fans who occupied the Kop, before it, too, was turned into an all-seated area, have a well-deserved reputation for singing their team's praises.

But I have two memories of beating them there when the Jungle moved, almost *en masse*, to Merseyside and out-sung the Kop. One of these was the Ron Yeats testimonial match and the other the European Cup Winners Cup semi-final. On both occasions the Celtic fans were in magnificent voice as they roared, sang and chanted their favourites on. I was there in the company of some English fans and both times they said the Celtic fans were by far the finest and the noisiest support they had ever heard. Coming from Liverpool fans, that was some tribute.

Pat Woods

Steve Chalmers will go down in the history books, quite rightly, for his late goal that won the European Cup, but the Quiet Man made many more contributions to the Celtic cause than just that one strike. Razor-sharp Stevie had lightning reflexes and was a real players' player who never hid on the park and always made himself available for the pass, even if it meant knocking his melt in to get to the ball and rescue a bad situation. He was also a tremendous example to youngsters coming into the game as it had not been easy for him starting out in football. He had to recover from a bout of meningitis, which curtailed his career, and, in fact, could have meant him calling it a day even before he had got to his beloved Parkhead. But his determination and never-say-die spirit stood by him well and he eventually made it to Celtic and to the Scotland international team, where he won five caps with the highlight being a goal in a 1–1 draw with Brazil at Hampden after which he swapped jerseys with the legendary Pele. A keen amateur golfer, he also had the honour of being champion at Cawder and was undoubtedly one of Celtic's finest ever ambassadors.

Hugh O'Donnell, Rutherglen

ONE game that will live with me forever is the return leg of the European Cup tie with French club St Etienne in 1968. They had beaten us 2–0 over there and, with a big travelling support, were confident they would march on in the Cup.

We were all in our usual spot in the Jungle enjoying an unusual 'cabaret' in the shape of a guy with a small monkey on his shoulder. The guy was a bit under the weather with drink but was not annoying anyone – at that time. The poor wee animal had on a Rangers jersey and we were all enjoying its antics, and it behaved itself well during the game. But when Celtic scored the third goal, to go 3–2 ahead on aggregate, the monkey's minder went berserk. Grabbing the monkey by its tail, he swung it round his head. Unfortunately the drink had affected his balance and he fell just as he let it go soaring over the heads of the crowd in the Jungle. The monkey was never seen again and the last we saw of the guy he was walking about looking under legs for his pet.

Tom Gallagher, Coatbridge

The Day I Lost My New Shoes in the Jungle

I NEVER thought I'd see the day when my wife thought my shoes were worth as much, if not more, than my life. Well that's not strictly accurate, but it's not far off the mark. I had gone with my mates to the Jungle for the European Cup Winners Cup semi-final first leg with Liverpool, in April 1966, and a crowd of 80,000 packed into the stadium for the eagerly awaited clash. The excitement was intense and the crowd kept surging forward at every attack, when suddenly all hell broke loose. The safety barrier had broken and we were all flung forward. It was bedlam and play was held up as we were all lifted clear of the pile of bodies on to the track. A number of us required medical assistance and, while I was getting first aid treatment I noticed my good shoes, bought only a few days before, were missing. In the excitement I had not even noticed but they must have been wrenched off as I was dragged clear. After getting myself sorted out and seeing Bobby Lennox giving us a one goal lead to take to Anfield (sic) – well I couldn't leave before the finish could I? – I got a bus in my soaking, stockinged feet and managed to get home. Word had spread about an accident at Parkhead and my wife was anxiously watching out of the window for me to walk up the street. When she saw me, shoeless and weaving my way up the street, she must have thought I was drunk. Chance would be a fine thing! Anyway, when I got to the door it took some convincing before she would let me in.

That was it finished for me, but not for my pal Hughie, who had been with us at the game. He, too, had been buried under the pile of bodies and when he did not report for work we thought he had been seriously hurt. His body hadn't been hurt, but his vanity had – for he told us on the phone he couldn't come in for a few days as he had lost his teeth in the stramash. He always was a vain so-and-so.

J. McVey

FOUR of us were walking down Springfield Road, *en route* from the Black Bull pub in the Gallowgate, heading for the big match, Celtic *v* Dukla Prague, European Cup semi-final 1967. It was a fine April evening and the 75,000 tickets were like gold dust. We were in jovial mood, having enjoyed a liquid refreshment, when one of my mates saw a window-cleaner pal working on the opposite side of the street. 'Have you not got a ticket?' shouted my pal, but the noise of the traffic must have made it sound like, 'Do you want a ticket?' for, within seconds, the cleaner was hurtling across the busy road with his ladder bouncing off car roofs, much to the annoyance of the drivers. When he found out it was an enquiry and not an offer, the window cleaner was none too pleased and we slipped off, leaving him raging in the street, with car drivers bawling at him, as we hurriedly left the scene. I am sure we were a lot more sober when we finally arrived in the park.

Eddie Burns, Maryhill

Joe McBride – King of the Goalscorers

I HAVE watched Celtic, man and boy, for almost 50 years and in that time have seen all the great players who have worn the hoops. Countless times I stood in the old Jungle, dodging the raindrops coming through the holes in the corrugated-iron roof, just to watch my favourites.

We've had some great players over the years. There was the trickery of Charlie Tully, a supreme entertainer, and Jimmy Johnstone, who had all the skills in the world. We had the greatest captain of them all in big Billy McNeill and a wonderful keeper in Ronnie Simpson. Bertie Auld and Bobby Murdoch ran the midfield with the efficiency of a Rolls Royce engine, and wee Bobby Lennox and Stevie Chalmers just ran, and ran, faster than anyone else I can recall.

But head and shoulders above them all was the King of Goalscorers – Joe McBride. Wee Joe was my hero. When you hear all the talk of great strikers in present-day football I have to laugh. None of them, and I don't mean to be disrespectful to the current crop in Scotland, could hold a candle to Joe. He proved his quality by starring with every club he played with – Kilmarnock, Wolves, Luton, Partick Thistle, and Motherwell – before Jock Stein made one of his shrewdest signings in bringing him to Celtic for just £22,000 in June 1965. Joe was an immediate success and became an instant hit with the Jungle fans for his goals – 31 in 30 league games in his first season. Then, unluckily, injury struck in Celtic's finest ever season, 1966–67, when Joe was at his mightiest. He never played after Christmas Eve yet finished the season with 35 goals – a record that speaks volumes for Joe's ability and goalscoring prowess. The song begs the question, 'When will we see his like again?' – in Joe's case the simple answer is 'never'.

Tommy Higgins, Baillieston

AS many Celtic fans are, I was born into the great tradition that surrounds the club. My grandfather, John, followed the side faithfully for many years throughout this country and Europe. Consequently, he became good friends with Jock Stein and many of the players that took part in the great European adventure of the Sixties. So it should be no surprise that my earliest memory of Parkhead and the Jungle is a European game. I'm not sure if Celtic *v* Sporting Lisbon in 1983 was my first ever game, but it's definitely a match that sticks out. I was in the stand that night and watched, with amazement, the antics of the fans across the park. Even at the age of eight, I decided that the Jungle was the place to be. Unfortunately, my father liked the idea of a seat and I was deemed too young to attend the holy ground on my own. For one reason or another I never made it to the Jungle until I was much older. But I had always enjoyed watching the celebrations from a different part of the ground. Finally my night arrived, and what a night it was. Celtic *v* Cologne in the UEFA Cup proved to be a welcome addition to the long list of great European nights at Parkhead. And I was in the Jungle! The whole place oozes Celtic. The passion and commitment of the fans echoes the trademarks of the team. Apart from that, the Jungle plays host to a tremendous, collective sense of humour. And in recent times that sense of humour has been badly needed with the team not enjoying the best of form.

Although the Jungle is now seated, the special atmosphere is still there and it remains the favourite part of the ground for me and many others. Hopefully, the legend will live on.

Austin Barrett

IT never ceases to amaze me the amount of rubbish that is left behind after football matches. Some years ago, before alcohol was banned from football grounds, I walked into Parkhead the day after an Old Firm game. The scene that met my eyes was incredible. The garbage had been gathered, but not yet lifted, and the piles were massive. I have never seen so many bottles. There were thousands and wee boys, who used to gather them in my young day, would have made themselves a small fortune. It reminded me of the days when a pal had told me he worked in Hampden Park, and after a big international he said the lads had filled 17 Corporation trucks with rubbish.

James Canovan

CHAPTER THREE

How it All Began – With an Annual Rent of £50

ONE of the most memorable days in Celtic folklore, certainly in modern times, revolves around the early hours of the evening of 25 May 1967, when Billy McNeill became the first Briton to get his hands on the European Cup. But another day in May, all of 79 years earlier, was of equal, if not greater significance, for it was then that the club, which we all now know as Celtic, began its very existence on its own ground.

In his book, *The Celtic Story*, Brother Clare (Dr James E. Handley) eloquently and stylishly tells of the formation of the Celtic Football and Athletic Club. Dealing with the origin and the early years, he tells of how the club, which had been the brainchild of a Marist Brother predecessor, Brother Walfrid, was formed to raise sums of money for charity. It was Brother Walfrid who had held out for the title Celtic FC against a strong feeling for the name Glasgow Hibernian. And the great man, who died in Dumfries in 1915 at the age of 75, was indeed happy when the new organisation purchased the ground which was to be its home.

A piece of ground stretching to half a dozen acres running east of Janefield Cemetery, Parkhead, was secured on 13 November 1887 for an annual rent of £50 and a group of volunteer labourers helped craftsmen to prepare it and turn it into a football ground for the newly formed club. With willing hands it took only six months for the pitch, measuring 110 by 66 yards, to be laid down, surrounded by a track 19 feet wide intended for cycling events and complete with an open-air stand to accommodate almost 1,000 supporters. A rough mound of earth surrounding the cycling track provided standing accommodation and there were two dressing-rooms with bath and toilet facilities. Spectators entered by one of nine gates in the wooden barricade around the ground and admission was sixpence for men, with women and, later, soldiers in uniform, allowed in free of charge.

All the work reached fruition on Monday, 28 May 1888, when Celtic, in white shirts with green collars and a Celtic cross in red and green on the right breast, paraded their skills for the first time on their new ground. The result was a happy one for all the workers who had slaved to get the pitch right for that day and they saw their team triumph 5–2 in a friendly with Rangers. Their fame must have spread quickly for, in the second outing the following month, a crowd of 6,000 saw them beat Dundee Harp 1–0, Brother Walfrid's dream was a reality and Celtic were on their way.

But things were not going to be easy: although matters on the football field were progressing very satisfactorily, financial matters were to present difficulties. The club members had to look after the cash diligently and the lease of the ground was to expire in 1892 when the landlord gave notice that the £50 rental would rise to £450. It was decided, quite rightly, they would have to look elsewhere for a new home and they fixed on a piece of waste ground, first on a ten-year lease and later to be purchased outright. This was situated between the original field and London Road but, again, there was much hard work to be done to get the place in order. Part of it had been a brickfield, half-filled with water to a depth of more than 40 feet, and it took more than 100,000 cartloads of material to fill in the holes and raise it to surface level. Again, however, volunteer labour was plentiful and on Saturday, 20 March 1892 Michael Davitt laid on the field the centre sod, fresh from Donegal that morning with a bunch of shamrocks growing on it.

By the middle of summer the new stadium held its first sports event, with its marvellous cycling and running track. The tracks were hired out for training three nights a week from 1 April to 31 August for one shilling and sixpence (seven-and-a-half pence) a month or five shillings (25 pence) per season for runners and three shillings (15 pence) or 10 shillings and sixpence (fifty-two-and-a-half pence) per season for cyclists. Around the track was a terracing constructed of wood, with steps three feet broad, ascending in a gradual rise to 12 feet or 18 feet above the surface of the playing pitch. The club had also erected, for shelter in bad weather, along the north side of the field, a covered stand 320 feet long – the largest in the country at the time – to accommodate 3,500 spectators.

They had to wait for the ground on the London Road side to settle before building a big stand. But, in the meantime, they built a construction of uncovered seating with a press box alongside. West of the covered stand on the north side was a two-storey pavilion, and this and the stand were built at a cost of £1,250. The ground in front of the covered stand was enclosed and terraced for patrons who were prepared to pay more than the ordinary admission charges.

Reaction was very favourable. The English League Committee members and J.J. Bentley, of the *Athletic News*, said the new stadium was far and away superior in almost all respects to any football field in Great Britain.

And that was how it got its name. For Brother Clare wrote: 'In layout and accommodation the new ground was such an improvement on the old stance alongside Janefield Cemetery that the punning remark of a supporter, likening the new conditions to a passage from the graveyard to Paradise, was seized upon by an alert newspaperman and the nickname "Paradise" clung to Celtic Park for many years.' The new stadium was given formal recognition when it was chosen for an international match with England in 1894, although it is said that Queen's Park tried to beat both Celtic and Rangers to the punch by offering Hampden free of charge, providing their members were admitted free of charge. The additional revenue came in handy for Celtic, however, and they were now able to make further improvements and replace the roof of the stand, which had been blown off in a winter storm. They were also able to provide additional seating, with more space for the press and telegraph services. The turf was completely replaced and the embankments enlarged with the wooden terracing on both east and west sides extended back to the barricades. The ground was now able to accommodate 50,000 spectators.

When the international was eventually held it attracted a crowd of 46,000, with takings of £2,600 – a record for a football match in Great Britain. This enabled the club to carry out more work on the rapidly developing stadium and the cycling track was laid down in terracotta with a banking of up to seven feet so that 18 laps comprised exactly five miles.

The south side still had no covered stand, although there was seated accommodation for 1,000 fans and a new banking was built the length of the field with the uncovered seating moved back to provide room for another few thousand spectators.

The international match of 1896 was again held at Celtic Park and the gates had to be closed half an hour before kick off with 57,000 spectators in position. The club had 100 policemen and 150 soldiers from Maryhill Barracks on duty and crush barriers were erected all around the park, with the banking on the north side raised to the level of the top of the covered stand. Seats in the covered stand were ten shillings (50 pence) for reserved and five shillings (25 pence) for unreserved. Admission to the covered enclosure in front of the stand was three shillings (15 pence), which included entrance to the ground. In those days reporters' copy was handled by a staff of 20 and a relay of a further 15 messengers to cope with all the telegraphic work. At that international match, four years before the turn of the century, 25,000 words and 800 telegrams were transmitted.

In 1897, four years before the lease was due to end, the first board of directors bought the stadium from the landlord, Sir William Hozier, for £10,000. The first directorate had consisted of Michael Dunbar, John Glass, James Grant, James Kelly, John McKillop, John H. McLaughlin, who was chairman, and John O'Hara. A meeting of the shareholders was raised to sanction the raising of additional capital to buy the field and a motion to raise £5,000 was agreed. A difference of opinion existed about the value of the new £1 shares with the directors being in favour of issuing them at 25 shillings (£1.25 pence). Finally, it was agreed to offer them to the current membership at par – five shillings on application, five shillings on allotment, and ten shillings when called upon. No outsider was allowed to participate.

Soon afterwards one of the directors, James Grant, decided on a financial exercise of his own and had built a two-decker stand on the site of the current main stand. This was his own, with rights to the revenue for a number of years, and was thereafter known as the 'Grant' stand. It was raised above the reserved terracing, acting as a roof to that section of the ground, and was extremely modern and well finished. It had a glass frontage and well-upholstered tip-up seating. The old press box was removed and erected on top of the stand, where it remained until recent years when the media personnel were moved into the main structure of the current stand.

Off the field, rivalry between Celtic and Rangers continued as they did their utmost to outbid each other in an effort to secure the right to stage future international matches before the Hampden Stadium was built. According to Brother Clare's *The Celtic Story*:

'One commentator offered a suggestion that was only heeded 60 years later. The commentator had written, "While rejoicing at the enterprise of the Celtic directors in improving the stand accommodation, one regrets that there is nothing being done for the enthusiast who can only spare a modest sixpence week after week. I think if a portion, say the east end of the ground, were roofed over it would be a boon to the spectators and a benefit to the club, for on a wet afternoon many stay at home who would go to the ground if assured of cover overhead."'

One of the most famous internationals held at Parkhead was the 'Rosebery' international in April 1900 and 60,000 turned out to watch Scotland beat England 4–1. The game was referred to by this title because the Earl of Rosebery had attended and made a speech to the crowd from the pavilion at the end of it, and the Scottish team wore his racing colours of primrose and pink hoops.

Talking of hoops, it was in 1904 that Celtic introduced the strip that was to become their hallmark throughout Britain, Europe and indeed anywhere in the world where football is played. Previously they had played in a jersey of green and white stripes but thereafter the hoops were there to stay. That season was also marked by a visit to the Continent, where they played four games with beginners in Vienna and Prague, and by a fire which wreaked havoc in the north stand, later to become the site of the Jungle, and most of the pavilion. The fire broke out in the morning of 9 May and the stand, with seating accommodation for 3,500 constructed of wood but with a roof of galvanised iron, was completely destroyed. Sparks from the blaze set fire to the two-storey pavilion nearby and the roof and upper floor of this building were ruined. Even the Grant Stand, the full width of the field away, was affected, although the fire there was discovered in time and quickly extinguished.

The north stand and pavilion had been built at a cost of £6,000 but the stand had been improved and strengthened at further expense on the orders of the Dean of Guild Court, after the Ibrox disaster in April 1902 when 26 spectators were killed and hundreds injured when the top of the huge west terracing collapsed. The stand and pavilion together had only been insured for £2,000 and while the pavilion was later patched up, the covered stand was eventually replaced by a covered enclosure which later became affectionately known as the Jungle. This structure was 300 feet long and 40 feet high and accommodated a few thousand spectators. At the same time the club took over the Grant Stand which, until then, had remained a private venture. Another fire features in the Celtic history as on 28 March 1929 a blaze wrecked the pavilion and all its contents, including the club records and photographs and other memorabilia. Fortunately, the cups, shields and other valuable trophies were stored elsewhere and not affected. But the team were forced to play all their 'home' games at nearby Shawfield. They could not look after themselves and the opposition in the Grant stand, as it was under demolition, but work was quickly begun and by the start of the new season things looked much brighter: the new stand would be ready for occupancy in August and the covered enclosure along the north side of the stadium had been given a roof.

Much later, in 1952 to be precise, three passageways were built at the Rangers end to help with crowd safety. Seven years later, on 12 October 1959, Celtic paid out £40,000 for the installation of a new floodlighting system and Wolves, at that time one of Britain's top teams, came north to hansel them. The 208-feet-tall pylons were claimed at that time to be the highest in the world.

Further improvements were made in 1966 when the old Jungle, which resembled an open-air barn, was torn down and replaced by a much more modern covered enclosure with a fine roof and a paved concrete flooring. The transformation was complete, but the name remained the same and the fans packed this area for every match. Work continued almost non-stop on refurbishment of the stadium and in 1968 the traditional Rangers end of the ground on the east end was given a first-class roof. And three years later, in 1971, further renovations were carried out on the stadium when the stand was given a new roof and other changes in structure gave it a capacity of 8,686, with the standing enclosure scrapped and seats taken right down to the touchline.

In 1985 more turnstiles were installed and exits widened at the north-west junction of Janefield Street, with much easier access to the Jungle. Under-soil heating was also installed. Then the following year the traditional Celtic end at the west of the ground was re-roofed, providing covering all round the stadium and, to coincide with the centenary celebrations, the total frontage of the stand was given a face-lift, including full extension work and new facilities incorporated. These included the building of the Walfrid Restaurant, plush lounges and boxes for corporate hospitality, a growing trend in modern stadia.

Despite the modernisation, however, there was still much talk of moving to a custom-built stadium at Cambuslang, but the fans displayed their disapproval at the thought of leaving their traditional home. And when Fergus McCann and Brian Dempsey staged their successful takeover bid in March 1994, it became patently obvious that Cambuslang was to be a non-starter and the hopes and aspirations of the fans would again be rekindled at their beloved Paradise.

THE management of Celtic have decided on a long-term policy of tremendous improvement and renewal of Celtic Park and its approaches.

The directors consider there are three priorities in tackling the job of creating a 'new' Celtic Park. These are:

1. Carparking facilities,
2. A new covered enclosure to replace that opposite the stand,
3. A new stand itself.

Negotiations have been going on for some time in connection with a new parking ground. Areas of ground in and around London Road, and adjacent to Celtic Park, would be ideal for the purpose, but a stumbling block is that this London Road district is scheduled as part of the Bridgeton and Dalmarnock redevelopment area.

The civic authorities are not unaware, however, of the fact that proper spacious carparking facilities for Celtic Park would be very useful amenities to the city. So provision in the redevelopment area of a Celtic carpark is under consideration. The directors hope that Glasgow Corporation officials and local representatives who are putting Celtic's case for new parking ground will soon devise a plan to suit all concerned.

Prospects are bright for the start of work on a new enclosure to take the place of 'the Jungle' before the end of this season. Two plans have already been considered by the Celtic Board. A third, which it is hoped will be the final plan, will be submitted and considered within a month. It is intended that work on the new covered enclosure will begin before the close season and that the structure may be half-completed before the playing season ends.

Celtic View, 25 August 1965

THE alterations to stadia which took place the length and breadth of the country in 1993 and '94 were the direct result of the Taylor Report following the tragedy at Hillsborough.

But there had been other changes made in the aftermath of the

Ibrox disaster which claimed the lives of 66 fans after a Rangers *v* Celtic match in 1971. One of these was at Manchester City's Maine Road ground when alterations were made to safeguard the fans and allow easier crowd dispersal at the end of the game. It stayed that way until 30 April 1994 when, coincidentally, the City's famous Kippax standing area, which held 30,000 and had been in use for 71 years, and the renowned Kop at Liverpool were packed for the last time. Both areas, where the most fervent fans of City and the 'Pool had stood, were demolished like the Jungle and replaced by seats.

And, like the Jungle and Kop, the Kippax was a place not without humour. Francis Lee, the former City idol and now chairman, writing in the programme on the last day of the standing area, recalled his relationship with the fans. Said Francis: 'I got on great with the Kippax. They had a chip at you and you chipped back. I remember a big, fat, red-haired bloke who used to torture us at the start of every season when it was boiling hot. He would lean over the wall, with his fat stomach showing, a bottle of beer in his hand, and leer at us and shout, "You're not fit."'

Manchester City Programme

THE Second World War was still raging in the Far East, although Europe had been settled for a month, when Ronnie Simpson, not yet 15 years old, made his début in senior football.

Granted, all sorts of chaotic things happened in wartime football, but it is still remarkable that a schoolboy found a place in goal at Hampden Park for Queen's Park against Clyde in the Summer Cup on 3 June 1945. Bobby Brown, later to become Rangers goalkeeper, could not be released from the Navy, and Queen's Park had been impressed by the young Simpson in a schoolboy cup final appearance for King's Park secondary a night or two earlier. So, in he went and Queen's duly won 5–2. Now a Queen's Park player and still an amateur, his next big moment came in 1948 when he was selected for the British Olympic Games team. Ronnie took part in the play-off for third and fourth place, which Denmark won 5–3. National Service then followed and after that Simpson turned professional with Third Lanark, playing with them for six months before moving to Newcastle United.

The St James's Park club, whose fans have much in common with those who stand in the Jungle, have been in decline for many years. But when Simpson joined them they were on their way to winning the FA Cup of 1951 and positively teeming with great players. Greatest of them all was Jackie Milburn, as deeply enshrined in Newcastle's history as McGrory is in the Parkhead psyche. There were also Scotsmen such as Frank Brennan, whom Simpson compares with Billy McNeill, Jimmy Scoular and Bobby Mitchell. It was a fine side and in 1952 Newcastle retained the FA Cup with Simpson in goal and gaining his first winners medal. This success was repeated in 1955, but thereafter the glory faded from St James's Park and by the early Sixties Simpson was back in Scotland, playing for Hibernian.

When Jock Stein arrived at Easter Road in 1964 there did not appear to be a great future for Simpson with Hibs and in September of that year he moved to Celtic in a low-key transfer which raised a few eyebrows for, although Celtic suffered chronic goalkeeping problems in the lean years, the 33-year-old Simpson hardly seemed to be the man to solve them. His career looked under threat again with the arrival of Jock Stein, the man who had sold him to Celtic. But he was thrust into the team in September and confirmed his comeback in the acid-test of a League Cup final against Rangers.

It was a strange game, a rough encounter, with Celtic leading by two strange penalties as Rangers threw everything at the King's Park goal. Those of us of a nervous disposition (in total about 50,000 Celtic supporters) behind the goal were reassured as we saw the slim, frail-looking Simpson taking command of the situation, exhorting full-backs Tommy Gemmell and Ian Young and calming down the excited Billy McNeill. Even when Rangers did pull back – it was yet another weird goal in keeping with the rest of the game – Simpson brought a note of professionalism to the proceedings which ensured a League Cup winners medal joined his two FA Cup badges.

From that point onwards Celtic, and Simpson, never looked back. Simpson won a Scottish international cap in the famous match when England were defeated at Wembley for the first time since their World Cup triumph. Then came the night of 25 May 1967 in Lisbon when Celtic triumphed over Inter Milan.

He played on for a couple of seasons but a bad shoulder injury, sustained in early 1969, effectively meant the end of a glittering and unusual career, the likes of which will almost certainly never be seen again.

David W. Potter, *Celtic Programme,* 17 August 1991

How the Jungle Got its Name

MANY people often ask me how the Jungle got its name and there are very many theories. As far as I am aware it only started being called the Jungle after the end of the 1939–45 war and it may well have had something to do with the troops returning from service. I always recall the other name of the 'cowshed', as it just looked like a barn with a corrugated-iron roof. But later it became known as the Jungle and was never referred to as anything other than that afterwards.

The best-known theory is, I suppose, because that was where the most vociferous fans congregated on matchdays and they certainly had a ferocious reputation. I remember doing some research and finding that Ian Ure, who was an uncompromising character and Dundee's international centre-half, was quoted as saying that some visiting players were frightened by the intensity of the Jungle's occupants.

But another popular and plausible explanation is that in the late Forties a lot of the Celtic fans had returned from the services, many of them having been stationed in the Far East, in places such as Malaya and Burma. Some people are said to have looked at the rather unkempt state of the Jungle at that time, with its earthen floor and leaking roof, and said it was like being back in the Jungle. That may sound corny but I suppose it is a feasible solution as to how it got its name. Anyway, it stuck and although it was a hazardous place to stand on rainy days, because of the leaks in the old barn roof, it was just as bad in warm, dry weather as the flakes of rust came off and stuck on your clothes and footwear.

No matter what it was like, though, and no matter what it was called, it was still a highly popular place to watch the football. But you always get the complainers and as recently as 1963, which was just three years before the original structure was demolished and replaced, a supporter wrote to the press saying, 'you need to be a balancing expert to stand on the terracings of the Jungle'. True enough, the steps consisted of earth with a wooden edge and where the wood was worn it was a bit hazardous. Until the latest modernisation, however, the Jungle had been much better with a fine roof providing shelter and with concrete terraces which provided a safe footing.

But even with the changes the name remained the same and it may take some time, if ever, before the new seating becomes known as anything other than the 'the Jungle Stand'.

Pat Woods

CHAPTER FOUR

Joe Ponsonby – King of the Jungle

THERE can be very few people who know more about the characters who lived their colourful existence in the Jungle than Joe Gallagher. Indeed, there can be few supporters who know more than Joe about his beloved Celtic and his loyalty to the Parkhead cause was recognised in 1968. On that occasion Joe was named by a Sunday newspaper as winner of their 'Mister Celtic' competition.

Joe remembers: 'I did not even know I was in the competition until I was told I had won it. It seems someone entered my name as they knew I had never missed a Celtic game for more years than anyone could remember and had even cashed in an insurance policy to get to South America for their World Cup play-off in 1967. But I was delighted to win it and it later opened doors for me to club functions.'

Certainly no one deserves it more than Joe, now retired after working, man and boy, for British Rail. Looking back on more than 60 years as a Celtic fan, the first of them as a nine-year-old in the Jungle, Joe has many memories – and loves recalling them: 'The old Jungle used to be packed out with characters. And all of them had nicknames that were like something out of a Damon Runyan book. "Tulip" Gallagher was one. He was so called because he sold flowers outside the cemetery. He was a distant relation and was quite a lad. Then there was one huge man called Yo-Ho, who was the leader of the Jungle choir. He got that name because of the call he gave out to the team every few minutes or so; he wanted everyone to join in and when you are his size no one argues with you. The chant of encouragement was then taken up by the Jungle and quickly ran round the ground. The patter around these guys was terrific and they, and others like them, were sufficiently good reasons for going to the Jungle. The fans used to gather round them just to listen to the crack. One guy was known as the Polly-Wolly-Doodle man. He got that nickname for shouting things like: "Look at that Rangers fan over there, he's got a face like a polar bear, polly-wolly doodle doodle all the day." He was the main man when it came to making up the songs and chants and he was great to listen to.

'But the undoubted King of the Jungle was big Josie Ponsonby, who came from the south side of the city. Josie carried a wooden staff that was the image of the one shown on the statues of St Patrick. He had carved it himself but it was so good a likeness that young curates used to run home to their chapels from the park to make sure St Pat's staff had not been stolen. Josie used to take up his customary place in the Jungle and hundreds of his followers would gather round him as he raised the staff as a signal to start the cheering. But Big Josie was out on his own: after a good result he would lead the fans, with his staff raised above his head, out of the Jungle and on to the Gallowgate. They would then march all the way to Glasgow Cross and down over the Clyde. It was a fantastic scene.'

Joe remembers that, in his youth, the fans who occupied the Jungle were known to all and sundry as the 'Mickey Masons'. He recalls, 'They got that nickname as they were professional people with the best jobs and good houses. They included in their number schoolteachers, butchers and self-employed men with a bob or two. They stayed in the more affluent areas of the east end, such as Dennistoun and Riddrie. And they were the ones who could afford to get right into the heart of the Jungle. In those early days you had to pay an extra sixpence to transfer from the ground into the Jungle and that was quite an extra expense. But when war broke out the iron and steel barriers were removed and the money raised sent to help the war effort. The Jungle was then an open area and I remember how the kids from the House of Correction, run by the Christian Brothers just off the Gallowgate, used to get marched in every other week. They were known to us other kids as the "Housey Boys" and they got in for nothing. I remember a couple of times me and my pals dressed up like them in their grey trousers and jumpers and nicked in with them. It was great fun beating the system, even as a kid.'

Joe, whose father, John, had taken up professional boxing to supplement his income, was actually born in Bridgeton in the east end but has lived most of his life in the Gorbals area on the south side. One of his earliest memories is of his first Old Firm game and Joe went there dressed in his new blue pullover, of which he was very proud: 'I was only about nine years old and did not realise the significance of wearing my new jumper that day. But it soon came to me when I got into the ground. I was hauled into the Rangers end by a big guy who obviously thought he was doing me a good turn. At that time the fans used to give wee boys lucky horseshoes to give to their favourite players. This big man gave me one and told me to run on to the park at a given signal and present my horseshoe to my idol. Little did he know I was a wee Tim. I ran on all right, threw away the horseshoe and then took off like a bat out of hell, straight to the Celtic end in the Jungle. A big polis chased me all along the track but the Jungle fans pulled me in to safety and raised the roof in a massive cheer at what I had done. That was in September 1930 and I'll never forget it, Celtic won 2–0 with goals from Bertie Thomson and Alex Thomson. A year later Johnny Thomson died after a collision with Sam English at Ibrox.'

There was a lot of poverty around that time in the east end and Joe remembers seeing fans gathering in their hundreds *outside* the ground to get in for nothing for the final 20 minutes. He says: 'I saw it a few times before realising what was happening. But it was a pitiful sight. The Jungle area was open and you could see out to the street where the fans were standing. Many of them were in their bare feet and stood patiently listening to the roars from inside before being admitted free of charge. I remember hearing that many of them had walked from as far away as Dundee just to get in for nothing to see their favourites. That's what I call devotion and it made me feel humble all those years later when I got that award for doing just what I loved – supporting my team.'

Apart from the time spent in the Forces during the war, Joe has rarely missed a Celtic match and was on first-name terms with all the great players over the years. Charlie Tully was one player he had a special admiration for, along with the McPhail brothers, John and Billy. Every member of the Lisbon Lions has a special place in Joe's heart but his extra special pick of that magnificent bunch was Jimmy Johnstone. 'They were a brilliant bunch of lads and marvellous players,' says Joe. 'I'm just a happy man that I saw them so often and also got to know them as men as well as players.' He goes on: 'I had four brothers and we all saw service in the Forces, but times were hard and we had only one suit between us. If we were home on leave

'They were my type of people,' Bertie says when discussing his vast army of supporters who packed into the north enclosure. And he was most certainly their hero as they showed on countless occasions during his long love affair with the club.

'The Jungle was *the* place for me,' says Bertie in a tone that dismisses any attempt at debate. 'I was lucky, I suppose, that we were on the same wavelength for that was where the bulk of the real support came from in my days at the park. When those guys got behind you it was a case of knowing you dare not let them down. Many a game they turned for us with their backing and I always set out to keep them going. If there was any wee trick I could pull during a game, I always tried to do it over there just for their entertainment.

'Mind you, sometimes it got me into bother with big Jock. I remember once we were playing Clyde and I had the ball and no one would come near me so I just sat down on it. The punters loved it but the Big Man nearly blew a gasket. He sent Neilly Mochan round the track to warn me of the dire consequences if I ever did that again. The Big Man thought I was taunting the Clyde lads and making a fool of them. There was no way I was doing that. It was just a wee bit of fun and the Clyde players realised that and joined in the laughter. But I should have known better than cross that Big Man, though, as he was very much the boss in those days and nobody ever got on his wrong side if they could help it. But that was just my wee gesture to the fans on what was the last appearance of the Lisbon Lions before we split up and the fans were there for a wee bit of entertainment and I decided to serve them something different for a change.

'That big man knew how to get the crowds in though. He was a pastmaster of pulling strokes. That game was on 1 May 1971 and in the previous game we had played Ayr United and Jock had fielded a team that was a mixture of the Lions and some of his promising kids who were on the verge of breaking through to the top team. In that game against Ayr the only men from the Lisbon side were Jim Craig, Billy McNeill, Jimmy Johnstone, Bobby Lennox and Willie Wallace. The others included Kenny Dalglish, Lou Macari, Davie Hay and George Connelly. But for the last game against Clyde the big man decided to do it in style and brought back the entire Lisbon side for the occasion, although Ronnie Simpson just ran out and then, at the kick-off, Evan Williams took his place. We won 6–1 with Bobby Lennox getting a hat-trick, Willie Wallace two, and Steve Chalmers the last one.

'Another time when big Jock pulled a fast one was once more

against Clyde when every Celtic player wore the No. 8 on their shorts to commemorate the club's eight successive championship victories; Again Lennox was the scourge of Clyde with another hat-trick in a 5–0 win, with Kenny Dalglish and Danny McGrain getting the other goals. The Celtic team that day, of 8 September 1973, was: Hunter, McGrain, Brogan, Murray, McNeill, Connelly, McLaughlin (Johnstone), Hood (Wilson), Dalglish, Hay and Lennox.

Auld, by that time, had left the Parkhead scene to go to Hibs. It had not always been plain sailing for Auld at Parkhead and Bob Kelly, who was chairman at the time, decided to do without Auld and transferred him to Birmingham for £15,000 in 1961. But you can't beat skill and ability, even although it was tinged, at times, with a fiery temper, and finally Kelly was persuaded by Sean Fallon to bring Bertie back to the fold. In his days with Birmingham, Bertie picked up a winner's medal when City beat arch-rivals Aston Villa to win the League Cup. But, as Celtic struggled, they realised how much they needed Auld's guile and influential midfield skills, and Jimmy McGrory signed him again in January 1965 for £12,000. It was a masterstroke for, within a couple of months, Jock Stein had arrived to inspire Celtic to a thrilling 3–2 win over Dunfermline in the Scottish Cup final. Bertie played a significant part in that triumph and he was welcomed back where he belonged.

He says: 'That was one of the best moves I ever made, although it cost me a fiver of a drop in my basic wage. But it wasn't a question of whether the money was right for me, the club was right and that was all that mattered. I was back to play for the team I loved and for the fans I loved.'

In those earlier days, when he had signed from Maryhill Harp in 1955, Bertie had made his mark on the senior players around him and these included such as Jock Stein, Bobby Evans, Bertie Peacock, Neilly Mochan, Bobby Collins and Charlie Tully. Charlie once said he noticed straight away that Auld was not like other young players who had joined the club around that time. 'He was full of confidence in his own ability,' said Charlie, 'and he used to lark around in a jockey cap and before I knew what was happening he was calling me "daddy".'

Although Bertie gave his very best at all times, the nights he loved most of all were the big European occasions when his big-match temperament came into its own. He milked them to the full and, to this day, the punters who packed the old Jungle still get a warm feeling of contentment when they remember how they saw the home-grown talent of the boy from Maryhill take on the highly paid stars of Europe and emerge triumphant.

EVERTON outside-right Alex Scott faced the Jungle as a Rangers star and now faces the Kop as a star of Liverpool's great 'across the road' rivals. Alex says: 'The Kop and Jungle are meat and drink to me. I'd rather play in front of them than in front of a polite, unemotional crowd. I'm fortunate that appearing before the big crowds, even if they are roaring for the opposition, always lifts my game. There is no doubt to me that the Kop makes more noise than the Jungle and it's a friendlier noise. It isn't so hostile, even when they are having a go at you.'

Alex Scott, *Weekly News,* 9 April 1966, before Celtic and Liverpool met in the European Cup Winners Cup semi-final

Young Explorer in the Jungle

IF ever anyone deserved a young explorer's badge it is surely seven-year-old Peter Johnstone of Drumchapel, Glasgow, who successfully navigated his way from his home in the west side of the city to his beloved Parkhead in the east. His father, James, tells the story well:

'I am (was) a Jungle person and have been all my life. I am now in my early sixties and for all the years I went to the Jungle I always stood at the same spot at the main passageway in line with the 18-yard box. In all that time I always took my children there with me to exactly the same spot every time. It was well known to my family and friends and everyone knew where to find me on matchdays.

'One day I was there on my own and at half time I felt a tug at my jacket sleeve. I looked down and was staggered to discover it was my youngest son, seven-year-old Peter. He had been with me to games a few times but on this particular occasion he had not been around when I left the house for the game. I had tried to find him before leaving but was told he had gone somewhere with a pal and I had to leave without him. I always travel by car and park in the same place near the ground. This was the only way Peter had ever been to the game with me so I was amazed at how he had managed to find his way to the ground considering we stay at the other side of town and he had never travelled by bus at all, never mind going alone.

'It turned out that when Peter came home that day and found I had left without him he decided he would make his own way there. Undeterred by the fact he would be on his own, he walked from Drumchapel to Anniesland Cross, a fair distance for an adult let alone a child. He then began looking for buses with Parkhead on the destination board but when he couldn't find one he asked a woman who directed him to the No. 58 bus stop. He got off at Parkhead Cross and set out to find my car where it was normally parked in Holywell Street. On finding the car, he knew at least that I was at the game, so he then knew where to find me in the ground.

'But I remain baffled at how he managed to get from west to east, never having made the trip other than by car. Needless to say I was, and still am, very proud of his achievement and his dedication to the cause to even try and make what was undoubtedly a daunting trip for someone of his age.

'As a supporter who stood in the Jungle all those years, I have never been back to my spot since they put a seat on it, and I never will. I've just found another spot to stand and goodness only knows what I'll do when they are forced to seat the whole place. No matter what they do, in my view at least, they will never ever replace that special atmosphere of the Jungle. And somehow my football will never be quite the same.'

CELTIC director Jack McGinn has an almost instant recall for the countless games he has watched from boyhood, first as a supporter and then as chairman. There have been many extremely proud occasions for Jack, whose love and enthusiasm for the club knows no bounds. But one in particular had nothing to do with a game, although it was yet another landmark for the club.

It was the first issue of the club newspaper, the first of its kind, on 11 August 1965. And it was soon to become essential reading for Parkhead fans. Jack, who had worked with Beaverbrook Newspapers in Glasgow, conceived the idea of a newspaper for the fans and was delighted to be given a loan of £600, after a board meeting, to launch his project. This was in March 1965 and, significantly, it was Jock Stein's first meeting since his recall to the club. Jack recalls: 'Jock received the idea with great enthusiasm and told me he would provide a picture of Celtic with the Scottish Cup for the first issue. He was true to his word and a 3–2 win over Dunfermline duly appeared as promised.' This was a remarkable achievement for Stein as his statement was made when the semi-final stage had still to be completed and no Celtic team had won the national trophy since Stein had led them to a 2–1 win over Aberdeen in 1954.

Jack's loan to set up the newspaper was rock solid and Jack said later: 'This was soon paid back and it was no bad thing either, for it made the paper stand on its own two feet from the start.' Still flourishing almost 30 years later, the *View* celebrated its 1,000th issue on 11 May 1988 in Celtic's centenary year.

Football is not the only sport, or indeed event, which has been watched from the terracings and stands at Parkhead. As far back as August 1897, Celtic Park staged the World Cycling Championships, attracting a phenomenal crowd of 45,000.

Moving forward to June 1913 a Hurling international between Scotland and Ireland attracted only a small crowd. But in September 1918, a crowd of around 12,000 saw a baseball game between teams representing the US Forces. The first organised speedway meeting in Great Britain was held on 28 April 1928 before an attendance of some 5,000.

The late, great Benny Lynch, Scotland's first world boxing champion, paraded his considerable fistic talents there before an audience of 20,000 on 2 June 1937. Benny lost on points to Irishman Jimmy Warnock.

Moving to modern times, one unforgettable occasion was the staging of the Special Olympics in 1990. An audience of more than 32,000 saw HRH Duke of Edinburgh declare the games open on July 21 1990.

And several major pop concerts have been held in the ground including the appearance of Parkhead fan Rod Stewart with Status Quo in June 1991 when 40,000 rocked the night away.

AT my age I feel I ought to know better, but I can't help making comparisons between the skills of the present-day players in the Premier League and the top men in the Fifties. Some of the so-called stars of today couldn't trap the ball to save their lives and, with very few exceptions, couldn't even spell dribbling, let alone do it!

Now when I think of players such as Willie Fernie and his skills it makes me weep and long for the good old days when players were skilled in every art of play. Willie fully deserved his nickname of 'King of the Dribblers' for he was truly the master. And he would be worth his weight in gold nowadays for his versatility. He was equally comfortable on the right or left side of the park, although he was predominantly right-footed and, as a result, we in the Jungle saw a lot of him close up. He was the man who made the team tick in that historic 7–1 win over Rangers in the League Cup final in 1957. And it was a sad day for the true football fan when Willie left Parkhead in 1958 to join up with the young Brian Clough at Middlesbrough. But he never really settled in England and we were delighted to welcome him back to Parkhead after just a couple of seasons. The game has changed beyond recognition since Fernie's days, with the emphasis now on speed and power, but I feel his skill would still make him a star of today.

Hugh McGonagle, Duntocher

LIAM BRADY was one of the best players ever to wear the hoops – pity it was only in his latter days when he was coaching the young lads in the reserves and not when he was in his prime. But he was proof of the pudding that great players don't always make great managers. I'll admit in the short time he was at Parkhead he had the team playing a neat, passing game that was at times terrific to watch but entirely without punch.

What annoyed me though, as a Parkhead diehard, was the players he got rid of who could still have been there doing us a turn on the park. I'm thinking of Chris Morris, Andy Walker, Derek Whyte, Joe Miller and Anton Rogan. And there have been more. Chris was a smashing player who knew when to use the overlap, like big Tommy Gemmell used to. Andy Walker's goalscoring exploits with Bolton have subsequently proved he still had a lot to offer and wee Joe and Anton gave us something you can't buy – love of playing for the jersey.

Tom Carroll, Uddingston

WE have been fortunate to have had some great goalscorers at Parkhead over the years. I never ever saw the great Jimmy McGrory in action, more's the pity, as he must have been a goal machine – averaging more than a goal a game with 410 goals in 408 league games.

But Stevie Chalmers and Bobby Lennox were my age-group and both were fantastic strikers. Bobby finally overtook Stevie in November 1973 and I think I am right in saying it was with a penalty against Dumbarton at Boghead. Just a pity it had not been in front of the Jungle, where they loved the speedy wee winger.

Mind you, talking of goalscorers for Celtic, you have to remember the exploits of others such as Joe McBride, Charlie Nicholas, in his first term with the club, and Brian McClair.

But another wee man must surely take a bit of beating. He is Dixie Deans, who was so good in the air he could hover like a bird waiting for a cross. I remember him putting six past Scotland goalie Alan Rough in November 1973 when Celtic won 7–0. He finished that season with 24 goals from 24 league games – some shooting.

Joe Brown, Motherwell

Following Celts From Russia With Love

TWO years ago I moved to Moscow with my new bride to work as a croupier in one of the many casinos there. Although we had problems getting a regular supply of food and the temperature hovered around minus 15 degrees and you couldn't get a decent pint anywhere, my biggest worry was not seeing Celtic. However, I did manage to keep up with the scores by phoning my parents every weekend. Our landlord used to bring our phone bill round and I had a terrible time trying to explain to him, in very poor Russian, why my telephone bill was ten times his monthly wage. The customs officials were very strict and opened nearly all our mail. I just wondered what they made of mine and if they realised why I was getting all the Celtic match reports sent to me.

We came home, for good this time, in December 1993, and my dad got two tickets for the Celtic *v* Rangers match on New Year's Day. I almost wish he hadn't bothered. First, my standing spot in the Jungle was replaced by a seat and the really sad thing was that I didn't recognise anyone sitting around me. My mates of long years' standing had gone. Okay, I know at times we had to stand in the freezing cold, had our views obscured by pillars, now and then fell off the crumbling steps in our excitement, and sometimes stepped in puddles. But all the time we had a powerful feeling we were part of a large and noisy family.

The death of the Jungle has, in my view at least, killed off a large part of the enjoyment of the game and for me it will never be the same again. That is why at only 26 years old I am now talking wistfully of the 'good old days'.

Gary Scott, Liverpool

IT was one of those turgid games when nothing seemed to be going right for anyone in the Celtic team. It was off days all round but, as usual, the fans picked out one man to voice their disapproval. To make matters worse it was pelting down with rain and it was Peter Grant's turn to get the heavy end of the stick from the Jungle. It wasn't his fault. It was just that somebody had to be the target for the abuse and poor Peter was *it* for the day. Now the Jungle fans know that Peter is a committed Celt and nobody, but nobody, tries harder for the cause, but that day the harder he tried the worse it got for him. His passing was awful and every time he touched the ball it seemed to go to the opposition. Then, during a particularly dull patch in the game, an eerie silence seemed to pervade around the ground. Then a voice from the back of the Jungle brought light relief to all. 'Taxi for Peter Grant,' he bellowed and within seconds the whole Jungle was laughing. I am sure if Peter had heard it he, too, would have roared with laughter. Talk about relief. It was of Mafeking proportions!

Tommy Leonard, Easterhouse

I HAVE very many happy memories of the Jungle from great games in Europe to super wins in domestic championships and Cup ties. But one of my recollections has nothing to do with either.

It was a game between the Scottish League and the Irish League – a fixture now long done away with. At that time, in the late Sixties, Rangers were struggling to win any awards because of the almost total domination of the great Lisbon Lions team under that master tactician Jock Stein. But they still had some very fine servants at Ibrox and Ronnie McKinnon was a solid stopper centre-half for them and he was chosen for the Scottish League side for this particular match.

At one point in the game the ball went out for a shy at the Jungle and as big Ronnie came over to retrieve it this wee guy at the front held on to the ball. Ronnie stood in the ash track waiting to get the ball and a wag from the back shouted to him, 'Hey, Ronnie, how does it feel to be on a winning side for a change?' Exit Ronnie, red-faced.

Tom Sullivan

IN more than 30 years of following St Johnstone, I have found Celtic supporters in general to be true football fans. They, more than supporters of any other club, have always appreciated good football, be it from their own team or the opposition. I recall going to Parkhead in 1969 and being unable to get back on the bus after the game because so many Celtic supporters wanted to shake our hands and tell us what a good team we had. I can also recall a match at McDiarmid Park a couple of years ago when Celtic were going through a bad spell and were losing at half time. Despite this, a large group of Celtic fans in the west stand had a ball at the interval, singing Christmas carols to the accompaniment of the Perth Silver Band.

St Johnstone Programme, 4 March 1994

Celtic have been very lucky over the years to have wingers who could play in the manner expected by the Celtic fans, who have always, in my lifetime anyway, put the emphasis on fast, attacking play.

I have been lucky in that I have seen the most modern of them all, Jimmy Johnstone, Johnny Doyle and Davie Provan. Johnstone was the greatest of all and it is sometimes forgotten that Jinky could score goals as well as make them. And at the same time provide fabulous entertainment. Johnny Doyle was one of the most committed Celts I have ever seen. He was not the biggest or strongest, but what he lacked in height and bulk he made up for in heart. And Davie Provan had style, speed and skill. His use of the ball was also excellent and I'll never forget his magnificent goal from a free kick to put Celtic back into the Scottish Cup final against Dundee United before Frank McGarvey dived to head a glorious winner. When Davie joined Celtic from Kilmarnock it was a right good bit of business by Billy McNeill. Unfortunately, his career was cut short by that ME virus when he still had an awful lot to offer football and Celtic.

Lawrie Grant

I WAS never blessed with any academic qualifications of any sort. I can always remember my first day at secondary school when the teacher asked, 'What are you going to do when you leave school, Peter?' I said I wanted to play for Celtic and the teacher said, 'But what do you really want to do?' After my first game for Celtic at Celtic Park my teacher was waiting outside for me. He came over and shook my hand and I said, 'I told you I was going to play for Celtic.'

Peter Grant, *Once a Tim*, issue 19

LIVERPOOL's fans are the more colourful but Celtic's followers are harder to play against. I've played before the Kop and in front of the Jungle when I was with Dundee. But since I've been in England, I feel the Liverpool sound has lessened. They've become so used to success they now take it for granted. Liverpool are the more light-hearted crowd. They've developed a kind of humour of their own. They can pick up almost any incident, any player, or referee and develop a theme tune. Celtic Park is the tougher ground to play at. I have known players scared to go near the Jungle to collect the ball.

Ian Ure, Arsenal centre-half, 1966

CHAPTER FIVE

Liz Taylor, Richard Burton, Rod Stewart and the Celebrity Celts

CELTIC FOOTBALL CLUB has always attracted more than its share of celebrity followers, stars from the world of showbiz, who have been taken by the club's style and total commitment to the spirit of true, top-quality entertainment.

Sean Connery, a megastar who knows all about style, has long been an admirer of the men in green and white and has attended many a match at Parkhead. Rod Stewart showed his passion for the club by introducing their name into one of his songs, 'You're in my Heart', which earned him a place in the hearts of Celtic fans world-wide. Rod is so much in love with Celtic that he even came to Parkhead to play in a game specially organised for him after he had missed out on the 'Last Day of the Jungle'. And Elizabeth Taylor and her then husband, Richard Burton, were so taken by the warmth of the reception they received from the Celtic fans in Budapest they asked to become members of a supporters travel group. None of them will have set foot in the Jungle, but all share an incredible depth of feeling with the fans and were readily accepted as kindred spirits.

In addition to this top-quality quartet, a number of world-famous celebrities attended the Special Olympics at Celtic Park in July 1990. The Jungle had never seen such a sparkling array of talent as film stars rubbed shoulders with royalty, Olympic and World

Champion athletes, international footballers, boxers and a galaxy of pop stars.

Hollywood megastar Warren Beatty, replacing Arnold Schwarzenegger who had to call off, led in the Scottish team along with Marti Pellow, the lead singer of pop group Wet Wet Wet. They were joined by an incredible list of top names at the head of the teams in a colourful parade of the countries as the Duke of Edinburgh officially opened the Games.

Eunice Kennedy Schriver, sister of the late President Kennedy and founder of the Special Olympics movement, told the athletes in her opening address: 'In an age of egotism, you have brought together under a single banner families, governments and commerce. You are the pioneers. And in our age of self-indulgence, your courage and generous spirits move us to change. You honour us far more than we could ever honour you.'

Celtic's own star Pat Bonner, on his return to Celtic Park for the first time since his heroics for the Republic of Ireland in the World Cup in Italy, was there leading the team from Ireland. Miami Vice actor Don Johnson led the USSR and was joined by his film-star wife, Melanie Griffiths, who led Estonia. Boxer Frank Bruno led in the English squad, Prince Raad led Jordan, and Prince Albert was at the head of the Monaco athletes. Others there included athletic champions Liz McColgan, Greta Waitz, Carlos Lopes, Olympic swimming gold medallist Duncan Goodhew, and Scotland's Grand Slam centre Scott Hastings.

Jim McGinley and his wife, Kathleen, are two Celtic fans who know all about the story of the famous night when Burton and Taylor donned Celtic scarves and tammies to become honorary Celtic fans. They masterminded it when Celtic visited Hungary to play Ujpest Dosza in the European Cup quarter final in March 1972. And for Jim, who had come from the steps of the Jungle many decades before, it was a dream come true. After graduating from the Jungle, Jim and Kathleen had started a travel business, 'Holiday Enterprises', and flew the Parkhead fans around the world in support of their team.

Jim, who has an almost photographic memory for all things Celtic, told me in great detail of one of the greatest nights of a lifetime of following Celtic: 'I knew that Elizabeth Taylor and Richard Burton were staying in the Duna International Hotel in Budapest and that Elizabeth had just celebrated her 40th birthday, when Richard gave her the diamond ring which was to become so famous in later years. We had booked 130 beds in the hotel for our European

Sporting Club and when we checked in, Kathleen wrote a note to Elizabeth and Richard inviting them to join us at the game the following day. Within half an hour the invitation was gladly accepted and they asked for rosettes and scarves, as well as match tickets. They also asked if they could go to it as real Celtic fans and travel to the game on the supporters bus.

'I spoke with Richard the next morning. I told him about the Celtic fans and how wonderfully supportive they were to their team, explaining that many of them had to save from one game to the next in order to get there on the big occasions. Some even gave up family summer holidays in order to fly to the European games and Richard was enthralled when he heard that these were ordinary fans and not the rich and affluent who could easily afford to fly the world. He was intrigued when I told him all about the fans who stood in the Jungle at Parkhead and he took an immediate liking to them, comparing them to his fellow countrymen from the Valleys who so fanatically support the Welsh rugby team.

'He and Elizabeth were so looking forward to the game but their hopes were shattered later that day when Richard phoned to tell me they were forced to call off as there had to be a retake of a scene from the film "Blue Beard". Richard "heard" my stunned silence at the end of the line and asked, "Will the fans be terribly disappointed?" I could hardly find the words to answer. Richard then suggested that maybe he and Elizabeth could meet the fans after the game for a "small party". The one condition laid down was that I should personally vet the guests but it should be for the fans only – with no paparazzi and no interlopers.

'That party is now part of Celtic's folklore and all our Celtic group met and chatted with the two world-famous stars who spoke as though they had known them all their lives. They posed for endless photographs with the fans and my greatest memory of that night was being given a close-up inspection of that 69.4-carat diamond and of singing to Elizabeth "You're Still the Only Girl in the World". Richard sang "I Belong to Glasgow" and caused great amusement with the line "I'm only a common old working chap". Ah well! Richard then offered to become honorary president of our European Sporting Club, which Kathleen and I gratefully accepted.

'My saddest memory is of losing the letter to Kathleen where Richard had joked, "Don't ever tell her I called her grannie". But one of my most personal, and warmest, memories of that great night is of Richard confiding in me that Liz had taught him the whole procedure of how to be a film star in contrast to his work on the stage of the theatre. "She could out-act me on the film set and she made me a film star," he told me. All these confessions from a world star to a wee man from the Jungle!

'One of Kathleen's fondest stories magnificently captures the wit of the Celtic fans. We had bought a bouqet (bedecked in green and white of course) and the youngest supporter there, ten-year-old Sean McKenna, presented it to Elizabeth. On the way home on the aircraft one of the fans asked Kathleen who had paid for the flowers. On being told we had, he immediately suggested a whip-round for the cash. Kathleen assured him this was not necessary but she was quckly told, "You have missed the point. If we all chip in I can go home and tell my wife I bought flowers for Elizabeth Taylor." We made the collection and kept a nominal sum, with the remainder going to Father Mullen for Carfin Grotto.'

ROCK superstar Rod Stewart has moved his countless fans world-wide with his music, but one of his outstanding memories is of the day he played before a mere handful of followers. It was the day he flew into Glasgow to play in a specially arranged match organised in his honour by his Celtic pals.

Rod, one of Celtic's most famous supporters, has been a fan of the club since the European Cup win in 1967. And some of the men who were part of that historic occasion in Lisbon were on hand to see Rod realise a lifetime's ambition by donning the hoops to play at his beloved Parkhead.

Looking back on that great day in January 1994, Rod says: 'I will forever be grateful to everyone who organised the game. It was fabulous to play at Celtic Park and it was made all the more memorable for me when I consider who I was fortunate enough to play alongside.'

His team-mates on that memorable day for Rocker Rod included his brothers, Danny and Bobby, plus Billy McNeill, Jimmy Johnstone, Bertie Auld, Bobby Lennox, Frank McGarvey and Dixie Deans. Ally Hunter, Tony Roper and Willie Haughey made up Rod's team with the opposition provided by Lou Macari, Jim Brogan, Tommy Burns, Roddie MacDonald and Jimmy Bone joined by groundsman John Hayes, who was later replaced in goal by Supporters Association member John Hughes, Paul Waterson, Brian Haughey and Jonathon Macari.

And, like the rock star he admires, Jimmy Johnstone will never forget that day and he has the souvenirs to remind him of it as Rod presented him with some of his gold discs – including one for Jinky's all-time favourite 'Maggie May' – in appreciation of a magnificent day. Jimmy recalls: 'That day was different class for all of us but particularly for me when Rod made that fabulous gesture of presenting me with those discs.'

Jimmy and Willie Haughey, the chairman of the Lisbon Lions' Testimonial Committee, were the men who masterminded the plan to allow Rod to fulfil his dream of playing in the hoops at Parkhead. Willie says: 'Rod had been keen to come and join the "Blow Away the Blues Night" but was unable to make the trip because of prior commitments so he phoned me and asked if there would be any chance of getting a wee game arranged for him instead.

'I contacted stadium director Tom Grant and when I outlined the idea he immediately agreed to provide the stadium for the match. I then got in touch with Jimmy Johnstone and what had started off as a wee kick-about for Rod blossomed into a big occasion as the lads were all keen to make it something really worthwhile for Rod instead of simply a knockabout. We soon made up two teams and, as well as those who actually played, we had Bobby Murdoch, Steve Chalmers and Danny McGrain along to join in the fun. It was a fantastic occasion and everyone had a marvellous time – especially Rod.' Rod says: 'What about my goal? I'll certainly treasure that memory despite the fact it had no bearing on the final result as we lost 8–3!'

The *Real* Fighting Men of the Jungle

PAT CLINTON has climbed many peaks in a boxing career that took him from the Celtic-mad mining village of Croy, Dunbartonshire, to the Los Angeles Olympic Games in 1984 and from there to the heady heights of being world fly-weight champion. But the Croy Golden Boy got as much fun, and no little thrill, when he achieved a lifelong ambition to play at Celtic Park. It made no difference to him that it was not a competitive game for the team he has supported all his life. Simply pulling on the strip and going out to play before a packed

Jungle was enough to send him home happy. The occasion was when he linked up for the Dukla Pumpherston team on the 'Blow Away the Blues' night at Parkhead before the workmen moved in to demolish the Jungle.

Boxers have a long association with Celtic Park, with most of them in spectating roles, but Peter Keenan, arguably the finest Scots fighter never to have been crowned world champion, is the exception. Peter remembers: 'I fought there a few times and always managed to draw good crowds. One occasion I remember clearly was in May 1949, the year after I turned professional. I outpointed Raoul Degryse, a tough Belgian, on the same bill Jake Kilrain retained his Scottish middle-weight title by outpointing Glasgow fighter Willie Whyte. That was a great night and there was about 15,000 there to see the bill.'

Crowds of that size, and much bigger, were nothing new to Perky Peter who, as well as fighting at Celtic Park, also carried his gloves to distinction at Firhill and Cathkin during a career that saw him crowned British, Empire and European bantam-weight champion and outright holder of two Lonsdale Belts.

I AM happy to say that not only was I a fan of the Jungle but I can almost claim to have been brought up there as I was taken there so often by my father, John, and uncle, Pat. The first memory I have of going there goes back to when I was five years old. I don't think I had even started school yet. And father used to lift me up and sit me on the wee shelf at the back of the Jungle. Older fans will remember that well as it was a common practice and kept us kids out of trouble and away from under the feet of the adults. It also prevented us from being crushed as the fans piled into the Jungle when the pubs shut just before kick-off.

Much later I remember being in the Jungle when there was a stramash when a goal was scored. I don't recall the actual game but it was a very exciting match and when Celtic scored the old Jungle almost rocked to its foundations. Suddenly, during all the jumping up and down with fans hugging each other, we were all aware of a wee man shouting 'watch my ear'. It turned out he had a plastic ear and it had been knocked off in all the excitement.

If it had not been serious for the man involved, it would have been hilarious as the Jungle, almost to a man, got down on their knees searching for the man's ear. The search went on for a few minutes and I am sure even the players wondered what the devil it was all about as a big section of the Jungle were seen to be down on their knees while the play continued. Finally, it was found and the wee man was delighted. It turned out he had had cosmetic surgery after being involved in an accident. But he stayed on until the end of the match before going home to get his ear refitted. After that I enjoyed many of the great games from my usual vantage point in the Jungle before graduating to the stand, where I now sit in comfort to watch the action. But I must admit to being a wee bit nostalgic when I heard the Jungle was being turned into an all-seated area. It made me turn my mind back to all those great days of my youth.

John (Cowboy) McCormack, former British and European middleweight champion

I'LL never forget one of my early visits to Parkhead soon after I had come over here from Ireland. I was only in the place a few minutes and I got an earful from the old Celtic-trainer Alex Dowdalls, who bawled me out for smoking in the dressing-room – and I've never smoked a fag in my life.

I had just arrived here from County Monaghan when I was just 17 years old and, although I had never heard of Celtic, or Rangers for that matter, I soon heard all about my fellow Irishmen like Charlie Tully and Sean Fallon at Parkhead. At that time I was still an amateur fighter and I asked permission to train with the players at Parkhead and was delighted when it was granted. Mr Dowdalls was a hard taskmaster and had us running up and down the terracings in big, heavy boots to strengthen our legs and build up stamina. Remember, now, at this time I was only 17 years old and in the company of senior players such as John McPhail, Bobby Evans and Neil Mochan. I had come to the big city from a village and was more than a shade naïve. But it did not take long to make me as street-wise as the rest of the city flymen.

But I admit I got set-up something terrible one day after training and even now I get a red face thinking back to my embarrassment. We had come in from a hard session and the lads decided to have a quick drag at a fag while Mr Dowdalls was out of the dressing-room. The cigarette was being passed round the boys when the door opened and in walked Alex Dowdalls. Someone, I honestly don't know who it was to this day, slipped the fag to me. There I was caught, almost literally red-handed, as I didn't know what to do with it. Mister Dowdalls smelled the smoke and looked round for the culprit. There were a few giggles as he came to me and said, 'I'm

73

surprised at you. A new boy just arrived and here you are leading the boys astray. You won't get far in the boxing game if you carry on like that.' I was left there mumbling, 'Honest it's no' me,' but he turned on his heel and walked out, leaving me open mouthed. The rest of the boys were falling about laughing but they later got me off the hook, although they never told the trainer who the real culprit had been.

I went back there many times, of course, to do my hard ground work before starting my sparring and, when my career came to an end in 1962 after I lost on points to Howard Winstone for the British feather-weight title, I often used to look back at the great days with such good pals in the Celtic dressing-room.

Derry Treanor

Paul's Jungle Gesture

PAUL MCSTAY has had some wonderful and unforgettable experiences in his time with Celtic and he is looking forward to many more. But his countless fans must have thought there was an impending parting of the ways in May 1992 when Paul raced to the fans in the Jungle and threw his jersey into the crowd after the last match, against Hibs.

Paul reveals: 'An awful lot was made of that incident and even now I find it hard to explain exactly what was going through my mind at the time. I know it must have been easy for people to read into it and imagine it had some sort of significance as it came when I was having long thoughts about my future with Celtic. But even now, years later, I must say it was simply an impromptu gesture, a way of conveying my appreciation to the fans for their support of the past ten years.

'They had been terrific to me in that time and, as I said at the time, there was an element of "just in case" about my gesture in throwing my jersey into the Jungle. The Celtic fans are, in my view, the finest supporters in the world, and I mean that from the bottom of my heart. My feeling that day, and it came on the spur of the moment, was simply to try and show them how deeply I feel for them. It could have turned out to be my last game for the club and if that had been the case I would have bitterly regretted not making some kind of gesture to them for all their backing over the years.'

The Jungle has played a vital part in Paul's career, for it was the place where his love of the club was nurtured when he was a schoolboy fan: 'Like everyone else I am sad at the changes made to the Jungle. That was why I was so glad to score in the final League game played in front of the Jungle fans. Those supporters in there had backed me all of my career and it was good to be able to give them something back on the last day. Mind you, it was a really nostalgic day, that 2–0 win over Dundee, for it saw the closure of a place that has always been inspirational to the team. And it was good to finish with a win for them. I'll never forget the scenes at the end of that game. The fans stood there singing for over an hour and they demanded the squad should come out to see them again. We did, and the sound of "You'll Never Walk Alone" made the hairs stand up on the back of my neck. Obviously I had heard it sung so many times before, but that day was something really special.'

Tommy's Tears and Souvenirs

TOMMY BURNS showed his affinity with the inhabitants of the Jungle by leaving them with many happy memories and not one but two souvenirs to cherish. He threw his boots in after his final match, against Ajax of Amsterdam, and his jersey in after his highly emotional testimonial match against Liverpool.

The elegant international midfielder enjoyed many glorious occasions in his 15-year-long career with Celtic but one that stands out in his memory was of overwhelming sadness – and it had nothing to do with defeat. It was that final appearance in the hoops against the Dutch masters and it got to Tommy to such an extent that it was, to use his own words, 'breaking my heart in the warm-up before the game even got under way'.

He remembers: 'I'll never forget that game with Ajax. I was determined to do my best, not only for those magnificent fans in the Jungle, but for everyone there. I also wanted to go out on a high note for personal reasons and when I saw the reception I got from the Jungle before a ball was kicked I was just broken up. I was running up and down in the warm-up with tears streaming down my face, but I thought at least if I do that then it won't be so noticeable as it will be when I leave the park.

'In the end it was one of those great nights but of tremendously mixed emotions. I was delighted to be getting the chance to say cheerio to the fans who had given me so much support over the years but sad I was doing it for the very last time. So when I was taken off I just ran to the Jungle and threw my boots in there as a gesture to the supporters who had given me their wholehearted backing during my entire career. It was an impromptu thing, just as it was when I threw my jersey into the Jungle at my testimonial match with Liverpool.

'The Jungle was the place where I had spent my youth at the park. It was magical, with fans who ate, dreamed and slept everything to do with Celtic. Their entire lives revolved around the club. During those two games, against Ajax and Liverpool, my thoughts were racing back to when I stood on the Jungle steps and cheered on my own heroes, guys such as Jimmy Johnstone, Billy McNeill, Bertie Auld and the rest. I was still there when Kenny Dalglish, Lou Macari, Davie Hay and others were the stars of the show at Parkhead.

'But when it came my turn to run out and face the Jungle for the first time I found it a truly incredible experience. When that part of the ground was packed, as it invariably was, it was an awesome sight and sound. It was such a contrast for me, having come from taking part in the cheering to be on the receiving end, and it was a rewarding feeling. I always counted it a privilege to have played for Celtic and to do it in front of that fantastic support is something I will never forget. Obviously, there are occasions that matter more to the fans than others, and they particularly enjoyed the Old Firm clashes and the thrill of facing Continental opposition. I am sure the sight of those fans and the sound of them in full voice must have scared the living daylights out of the foreign players.

'The Jungle had such an effect on me that I was always better pleased when we played down that side in the second half as the fans were able to lift me if necessary. And when I scored, which was not too often, I always ran straight to the Jungle to celebrate. I think

it was the fact that I came from there myself that made so much difference to me.'

IT was not a season of glory all the way. We could look back on the
Championship victory, and that would be more than enough for any
other team in the League, plus success in the Scottish Cup, but this
was tempered by the disappointment of failure to make it six successive victories in the League Cup. And for me, as someone who
always looks beyond domestic football, to the even greater failure in
the European Cup.

I put forward no excuses for our League Cup defeat by Rangers
in the final at Hampden. We had stumbled in the semi-final against
Second Division Dumbarton, and our form did not rise to the heights
demanded of a Cup final when we met Rangers. It was a game which,
on the day, Rangers deserved to win for we never put them under the
pressure which has become the trademark of Celtic's success.

In the European Cup we paid the penalty for two easy draws
in the opening rounds, against Kokkola of Finland and then
Waterford. I will not deny that, at the time, these seemed to suit us
for we were faced with a heavy domestic programme. But when we
played the quarter-final against Ajax of Amsterdam, the eventual
winners, the team were not tuned up to the very high requirements
which the European Cup demands. We held Ajax comfortably for an
hour and then came the collapse and we lost three goals, an almost
impossible number to pull back. Although we did score once in the
second leg at Hampden, we had left ourselves with too much leeway
to make up. I have a dream to keep Celtic at the top, despite the tran-
sition which any team has to overcome. But I realise it will not be
done without a lot of hard work and also the support of you, the
fans. No matter how successful we have been, we still need that
support – especially the youngsters, who may need time to fit into
the pattern of the side.

If these pieces all slot together I am confident Celtic can go
ahead to conquer the new soccer world as successfully as we have
in the past.

Jock Stein, in his manager's report in the *Celtic Football Guide* for
season 1971–72, referring to season 1970–71

IT didn't take me long to find out the true strength of Celtic's fabulous support and it is something that I will never forget. I had just

arrived at the club and we were playing Arsenal at Parkhead in a pre-season friendly and, to be honest, they were much better prepared than we were. They steam-rollered over us but our marvellous support just kept singing and roaring on the lads. But it was only when Paul McStay scored, with a screecher of a shot, that I got my eyes well and truly opened. From the roars that greeted that goal you would have been forgiven for thinking it had been the winner instead of just a goal to take the bad look off a heavy defeat. It was a magnificent reaction and I thought then that these people had to be something very special.

Two other incidents underline that fact for me. The first time I was at an Old Firm game, first as a spectator and then as a player, I had never, ever heard such depth of feeling. It just hit you from the minute you walked out the tunnel and saw the massed fans in the Jungle. That feeling will stay with me forever and it is one football memory I cherish.

The other occasion was when I came back to Glasgow for the 'Blow Away the Blues' night when they were getting ready to seat the Jungle. I didn't honestly know what to expect by way of a crowd for that night as, after all, it was not as though it was a real live competitive match. It was between two sets of teams who had been, in their day, the real trendsetters – the Lisbon Lions and the Manchester United team who followed them in winning the European Cup the year after Billy McNeill and his men. That, plus the fact it had rained all day and into the evening, I thought would have trimmed the attendance. Just shows you how much I knew of these great fans as almost 20,000 turned out to salute the teams and to say farewell to the Jungle. It was an incredible night and, to make it even better, I got a game to ensure it was a night to stay with me for the rest of my life.

Mick McCarthy, former Celtic and Republic of Ireland central defender

THE Jungle was the place I always ran to and saluted when I took the field at Parkhead for they summed up for me the real feeling of Celtic. It made such a staggering difference to me because when Billy McNeill brought me to Parkhead he gave my career the kiss of life. I had been stagnating with Sheffield Wednesday and it was so bad that the fans there gave me a tough time, even when I was out warming up to come on. Then came the transformation when Billy signed me for Celtic. I joined a team that was surging into the history books by winning the Scottish League Championship and Scottish Cup in its centenary year.

I loved the fans, the whole way of life, and we quickly settled into a rapport that lasted all the time I was there. Into the bargain Jack Charlton heard reports of my play and brought me into his Republic of Ireland plans, which was a massive bonus. I will never be able to repay the Celtic fans for the part they played in helping me to achieve the success I have.

Chris Morris

I WELCOME challengers. That is not just an empty close-season state-ment. It's obvious that if there are more teams really competing for the Championship, then the quality of football will rise, the excite-ment will be generated in areas all over the country.

Jock Stein, in his manager's report after Celtic had won their eighth successive league title

Jock Stein was the master when it came to innovative ideas to keep the fans, players and the media on their toes during the great years of nine-in-a-row. But he surpassed himself when Celtic met Clyde in the first home game of the League campaign in season 1973–74.

Every single member of the team wore a number eight on his shorts to commemorate Celtic's marvellous feat of having won the Championship in eight consecutive season. The team that day was Hunter, McGrain, Brogan, Murray, McNeill, Connelly, McLaughlin, Hood, Dalglish, Hay and Lennox.

Matt Brown, Rutherglen

MY wish for Celtic is that they, and all the other clubs, could get back to the days when boys were encouraged to come to the football by being lifted over the turnstiles. That certainly happened to me and, I am sure, to countless thousands more many years ago, and as the old chairman Robert Kelly (later Sir Robert) used to say, 'the young-sters are the lifeblood and future of the club'.

I was born and brought up in Society Street, Parkhead, just a few minutes walk up Holywell Street and into Janefield Street behind the Jungle. Just like a lot of other wee boys of my age in the

Thirties, I used to stand outside asking to be lifted over. I was never disappointed. But I was one of the lucky ones, having a family to look after me – a father, mother and sisters. Others were not so lucky and I remember seeing groups of kids being marched in double file along to Parkhead from an orphanage in Comeleypark Street in the Bellgrove area. Sometimes there would be as many as 50 or 60 boys in pairs and they were always well behaved as they walked to and from Celtic Park. They were always admitted through the season-ticket gate in Janefield Street and stood in line along the wall at the front of the Jungle. At the end of the match they waited until they were brought together and walked back to the Home. I often wonder if any of these boys are still living and if they still go to Parkhead.

Jimmy Roberts, Chapelhall

THIS season brings a new League set-up with the Premier, the First and the Second Divisions. The old system had, over a number of years, given too great a disparity between the leading clubs and those at the bottom – a disparity which gave us a large number of games with minimum spectator appeal. This can hardly happen this season. While the above is obviously true there are other factors which could tend to act in the opposite direction, such as clubs in the Premier League playing each other four times instead of twice and the effect of increased competition, which might tend to induce a greater defensive strategy. Whereas these two points are also true, it is felt that something had to be done to help bring support back to the football ground in the numbers of the past. It is also hoped that the new Premier League will equate more with the English First Division in that it might be possible to retain, in the Scottish scene, some of the stars who would have taken the road south and so on the field of play to improve our own standards of football. I hope that Scotland's international team will be able to draw more heavily on those stars who are playing in Scotland rather than choose from the Scots in the English League.

We must congratulate the Scottish Football League clubs which have shown the flexibility of thought to allow this new pattern. We all sincerely hope the new system will be an outstanding success – however, if not, we must still retain that flexibility of thought to allow us again to change.

Desmond White, chairman, in the *Celtic Football Guide* 1975–76

I SUPPOSE I am very lucky to be here to tell you the story of how I almost became a statistic in what could have been a football disaster. It happened in season 1968–69 after Celtic had beaten Rangers 1–0 and the crowd were leaving the Jungle to enter Janefield Street, singing and dancing after our heroes had beaten Rangers. As we approached the main gates someone in front of me tripped and fell. The crowd swayed towards the supports between the gates and, by this time, several more people had fallen to the ground. There could have been a full-scale panic but the fans were doing their best to stay calm. But the mood had changed from one of extreme happiness to fear. The pressure of the crowd behind, who did not realise what had happened, was intense and I was brought down as well. One of my friends, who was just behind me, quickly sensed what had happened, as it only took seconds, and started to drag people off me. We were in grave danger of being suffocated but luckily for me my pal, Big Pat, forced his way to my side and grabbed me by the neck and hauled me clear of the pile of bodies. Fortunately, by this time the crowd had realised what was going on and held back to allow everyone to scramble clear. It took only minutes, I suppose, but it felt like hours before my head was clear again. I shudder to think what might have happened if it had not been for Big Pat.

Kenny Hughes

TO avoid this particular Rangers player any embarrassment, I'll not name him – but this is true, honest. I was in the Jungle when this boy blue came over to get the ball for a shy. A guy looked right up at him and said: 'Hey son, you're so ugly your mammy must have had to have venetian blinds fitted to your pram.'

Big Kenny

I was at the Celts for Change victory night after the board changes in March 1994 and it was like the celebrations after we had won the Centenary Double. Now, with all our troubles behind us, I hope we can march back to greatness.

Charlie Brown

JUST how successful the *Celtic View* has been, as it enters its fifth season, can be ascertained from our steady circulation of 27,000 copies each week. It is also worth mentioning that copies of the

CHAPTER SIX

The Law *in* the Jungle

'ALLO, 'allo, 'allo, this recollection of one of Celtic's most historic nights for new boss Billy McNeill and his team is just too good even to think about editing. It simply has to go in unaltered. And the writer, a serving policeman, even had the foresight to supply his own heading: The Law *in* the Jungle. There's no way I would even think of changing that. He writes:

'One of the perks of being a Polis in Glasgow is getting the chance of working overtime at football matches and, with a bit of luck, you might find yourself getting paid for watching your favourite team. That happened to me on very many occasions, but one of the most memorable was the Old Firm match at the end of season 1978–79. It was manager Billy McNeill's first season in charge and at the end of a dramatic term he found himself needing two points to win the league. Arch-rivals Rangers, however, were also very much in the hunt, needing only one point for overall victory.

'At that time I worked on the north side of the city and a few days before the big decider my sergeant, who was a big bluenose, told me, "You've won a watch wee man, you're working at the game. Now do you want the *bad* news? So am I, and I'm going to enjoy watching your team getting stuffed." The cop I worked with was also a Celtic fan and was told that he, too, was working at the match, but the chance of us working together was remote to say the least, if not impossible.

'On the evening of the match the atmosphere in the city was

83

electric, much more so than I had ever experienced. There had been a build-up of tension for several days as the season hinged on this one result for both Celtic and Rangers. Anyway, when I arrived at Celtic Park I was told right away where I was working that night and I honestly could not believe it. Me and my pal were paired together and we were working in the North Enclosure – the Jungle. It was unbelievable, incredible, fantastic – for this night we hoped would be one to remember.

'As we stood there, keeping an eye on the crowds arriving and listening to the songs and the patter of the fans in the Jungle, the excitement was growing by the minute. We could sense this was going to be an extra-special occasion. Suddenly, I was aware of a presence behind me and it was our sergeant. He resembled the 'Honeymonster' in the television adverts wearing a Polis uniform – all six feet six inches of him. "Right you two, nae jumpin' up and doon when the Gers score," he joked. Well I took it to be a joke anyway whether it was or not. If it was, it was his first. He had a strange sort of face. He was a huge man and his face fitted in with his size. But he wore a permanent frown like an undertaker and only his lower chin moved up and down – he reminded me of a character in the kiddies' TV show *Captain Pugwash*.

'It wasn't long before the street-wise characters in the Jungle realised me and my pal were Celtic fans. It must have been our angelic smiles, or maybe it was that we were joining in their singing – miming of course! Tomorrow we might have to give them the jail but for that night an amnesty was in place.

'The first half was a disaster and is better off left at that, with no colourful descriptions of the action. But soon the second half was underway and Rangers were a goal ahead and that great evergreen Celt, the late Johnny Doyle, had been sent off. But ten-man Celtic buckled down and fought back quickly, stepping up a gear. Roy Aitken equalised and shortly after that George McCluskey scored to put Celtic ahead 2–1. The excitement then was fantastic, one of the best atmospheres I have ever experienced at a match.

'Well I suppose that's when we were noticed, my mate and I. Let's face it, the punters in the Jungle don't often get the chance to throw the Polis up in the air. But this was different, especially when they knew that the Polis they were throwin' about were just as ecstatic as they were about the score at that time. Once we managed to get our hats back from a wee wummin' – who said they would keep the neds away if she hung them in her hallway – we were told by one of the Jungle fans that our sergeant was trying to attract our attention.

There he was, out there on the track, pointing at us like Kitchener on the war posters. We were beckoned over to see him and, as we went, everybody in the Jungle started to sympathise, shouting, "Sergeant, Sergeant, leave them alone!" This just made the big bluenose even worse. He was seething. And the Celtic fans were shouting, 'Best of luck, tell that sergeant where tae go and we'll see youse at the next game."

'No luck. As we stood there before him like guilty men awaiting the verdict, we were given a lecture about letting the force down, etc. Then he delivered his judgment: "Make your way to the junction of London Road and Springfield Road, points duty." We were shattered. Right in the middle of the most important match for ages. As we walked away, slowly, he shouted after us, "I'll see you both in the morning." It sounded ominous.

'Anyway, we took the long way round the track, hoping to savour the atmosphere a wee bit longer. Tomorrow was another day. Right now we were winning and we wanted to make the most of it. Besides, there were no motorists about, everybody in the east end was at the game, or so it felt at the time. As we approached the dugouts I glanced in at the Celtic backroom staff. Huge smiles were on every face – although you could still feel the tension.

'Then it all changed in a flash. In the few short strides it took us to actually pass the dug-outs Bobby Russell made it 2–2 and all to play for again. It was going to be one of those nights. We walked out of the park and into the carpark. It was like night and day, all quiet outside the ground and bedlam inside. "Points duty at London Road and Springfield Road, I still cannae believe he would dae this tae us," groaned my mate. But the big sergeant could, and he had, and we were out – away from the big decider just at a crucial time. It was desperate. What we suspected was true. London Road junction was like what they say about Aberdeen on a flag day – dead. As we stood there having a post-mortem on the night's events and wondering what awaited us in the morning, an almighty roar ascended into the night sky above the park. It meant only one thing: somebody had scored. But who, how, and for which team? we wondered. Even the songs that filled the air minutes later failed to determine the answers for us, for it was just a massive ear-bending babble. Just then a Rangers fan came running along London Road from the park.

'"Who scored?" I enquired, trying to keep my voice as impartial as possible – this was not easy under the circumstances, I assure you.

'"Jackson," he replied, "Colin Jackson."

85

'Me and my mate just looked at each other. I swear we could both see each other's blood just draining away. All this and points duty and facing the sergeant in the morning, to say nothing of the abuse we would take from our other colleagues. When will all this pain end? I thought. But the Rangers punter had not finished; still running, obviously trying to get as far away from Celtic Park as possible in the shortest space of time, he shouted over his shoulder, "Aye, f....... Jackson. An own goal, the big stupid b........"

'Me and my mate went daft. Like wee boys we celebrated by jumping up and down, hugging each other in the middle of the road – empty, thank God, although at that time we weren't caring. When I think of it now, though, if our sergeant had seen us then it would not have been London Road points duty, it would have been Siberia – if they have road junctions in the salt mines.

'It was still not over, however, and minutes later another roar blasted the night air – but this time we soon knew what had happened as a tidal wave of Rangers fans poured out of the stadium. The streets were flooded in blue and white scarves *and* the tears of the fans. They were inconsolable. A point would have done them and made them champions. But the unthinkable had happened and they had lost. This time it took a wee bit longer to find out who the late-goal hero was, as no one in blue thought to volunteer the information to two beat cops on points duty. We later found out Murdo MacLeod was the man whose late goal had made victory certain and we had won the League.

'It was another hour before we were told we could go home and, as we both stood in the Gallowgate waiting for a bus, a supporters' bus drew up alongside and a happy Celtic fan leaned out and said, "Where to, boys?" Incredible as it may seem, from that crowd of 52,000, it was one of the lads from the Jungle who had thrown us up in the air a few hours earlier. The bus sang its way through the east end before they dropped us off, hurrying home to see the highlights on television. Unfortunately, there was a strike, or something, at the studios and we never saw the goals until much later when we saw it courtesy of Celtic Films. Maybe that was a blessing in disguise as you might have seen more than the goals. The Chief Constable and my mother – and I don't know who I feared most – would have seen me and my pal being thrown in the air and then shown the Polis equivalent of the red card. *What a night!*'

Name and Rank withheld (in case we are up for promotion – somehow I doubt it).

Maggie's First Night in the Jungle

IT was another wet and windy night at the old ground, but I consoled myself by saying at least I was getting paid overtime *and* getting the chance to see my team. Now, sometimes it can be very boring standing there, or walking around the track as we used to have to do, and listening to the conversations was as good a way of passing the time as any until the action started. This particular night the Jungle choir was in good voice right from the start of the game, but there had been a lull before the hordes arrived to take their places and I was conscious of a young lad and his girlfriend pushing through the crowd to the front of the Jungle. It soon became obvious from their chat, that this was not only her first visit to the Jungle but also her first visit to a football match. The conversation was magic:

'Thanks for bringing me to the gemme Wullie. I'm fair excited.'

'Nae problems,' said he. 'Ah kinda thought it was your first time here when I saw you wearing your stilleto heels. Never mind, enjoy the game, Maggie.'

Celtic lost the toss and were forced to play into the wind and rain and, as the game went on, Wullie started to join in the singing with the Jungle choir – except for the times he had to stop to answer some of Maggie's enquiries regarding the rules of the game. As I stood there trying to keep an eye on the crowd (honest, Sarge!) and with one eye on the game, too, I was still conscious of the young lovers. Maggie was clearly infatuated by Wullie and was hanging on his every word.

'Wullie, you really know everything about the game, don't you?' she said.

'Ah well, you pick it up as you go along, doll,' said he, but Wullie was clearly getting anxious as, with five minutes to go to half time Celtic had made no real impact on the game and the wind was so strong it was difficult to string passes together. The fans were getting restless.

So, too, was Wullie when Maggie asked, 'When are Celtic going to score, Wullie? I thought you said they were a good team.'

Poor Wullie, I thought. But he was doing his best to remain calm, although he must have been questioning the wisdom of having brought Maggie on this great night out. 'Look, Maggie,' he said, 'there's nae sweat, we'll have the wind in the second half.'

That was it. Maggie went silent. She was obviously dumb-founded by this piece of specialist information from her amateur weather-expert boyfriend, who was something of a Michael Fish as well as a football know-all. What I, and Wullie and every other fan within listening distance did not realise was that Maggie was unaware the teams changed ends at half time and would be kicking in the opposite direction. I glanced over at her, for it was the first time she had been quiet since they came in and the poor soul looked as though she had been caught up in a Jungle time-warp. Then she broke her silence, looked at her hero, and uttered the immortal words, 'Oh Wullie, you're magic. You even know that the wind's gonnae change direction in the second half.'

The Jungle collapsed laughing. Maggie, if you are still out there – nice one!

Bob Ramsey

Watch that Wean!

IT was quite a nice night for a football match, I remember thinking to myself as we prepared to line up on the track. I had only been on the job for three months and was still finding my feet as to how policing a big match should be done. It was my first time on duty right in there where it all happens – the Jungle – and I could still hear my sergeant's instructions, 'Remember and keep the passageways clear.'

The ground was starting to fill up rapidly and I was kept busy walking up and down the passageways shouting to the fans, 'Keep in there lads.' 'Get off the stairs.' 'Move in a wee bit more.' 'Watch that wean.' 'Look, sir, I'll not ask you again, will you please get in off the stairs.'

I pleaded and I begged. I cajoled and ordered. But would they move? No, sir. I wondered what the answer was until I noticed, out of the corner of my eye, Old Wullie. There was nothing Wullie did not know about police work. He seemed to have been on the force for about 100 years. What he didn't know about working the street was not worth knowing. He saw how uptight I was getting and quickly took me on one side for some much-needed advice. It was one of the best tips I have ever heard.

'I'm going to show you the best crowd controller ever invented, son,' he said, 'My mother-in-law gave me this years ago and, guess what, I've got one for you,' said Wullie producing the secret weapon from his tunic lapel. It glistened in the night under the floodlights. It was just short of six inches of steel and as sharp as a tack at one end, with a beautiful pearl stud on the other – *a hat pin*! 'Now, son, here's yours. Just the slightest of jabs is all that is required. Follow me,' said Wullie. He then started to push the punters on to the terracing and off the passageway. 'Come on, lads, clear the passageway,' was his cry and, like the parting of the Red Sea, it worked. I watched him going about his task and Wullie had it down to a fine art. Any fan who was troublesome or started to argue with him, suddenly jerked and jumped back as though they had been given an electric shock. 'Oh, ya bass,' was only one of the shouts I heard, but it was used most often. Within seconds the passageway was clear. 'Now, remember, son, don't jab at the lads, there's nae need for that. Just a wee nip is all that's needed,' said Wullie.

So, remember the next time you see a picture of a football ground that looks nice with all those neat straight lines down passageways, just think it might be me and *my* apprentice just doing our job. Right, Wullie?

Black Bob

I FEEL aggrieved for the fans losing the Jungle for that was *the* place with the atmosphere. Teams used to worry themselves sick at the thought of running out towards the Jungle.

Peter Grant, *Once a Tim*

CELTIC PARK never had a big stadium clock to my knowledge, but that did not prevent the players from knowing how long there was to go in the game. They had their own way of keeping tabs on the game for, with 20 minutes to go, the big gates would be thrown open, allowing people in free of charge.

When times were hard this was the only way some fans could get to see a game and sometimes this scheme worked to the advantage of the players as they knew if they had to raise their game in the closing stages. That must have happened a few times I am sure, and I remember one Cup tie in particular when Celtic were trailing Motherwell 4–2 when the gates were opened. It was the quarter-final of the Scottish Cup and Celtic battled back to level at four all. The scorers were Crum (2), Lyon and Buchan. Celtic went on to win the replay 2–1 at Fir Park with McGrory and Buchan the scorers. Celtic then beat Clyde 2–0 in the semi-final at Ibrox and Aberdeen 2–1 in the final at Hampden.

Jimmy Roberts, Chapelhall

I lived in Palace Street, Parkhead, just off Janefield Street, for 20 years from 1943 to 1963 and spent most of my time in the Jungle. After all, it was almost on my doorstep and I could be in the park minutes after leaving my house. During that time there were some great moments but also some I would much rather forget.

I had worked as a scaffolder in the shipyards and was made redundant in 1964. But I got myself a job in the stuffy old Post Office sorting office in George Square. The only consolation for me was that I finished at 1 p.m. when on early shift and the lads were busy putting up the towers at Celtic Park for the floodlights so I used to wander into the park to watch them. The skill of those steel erectors was terrific and I never ceased to wonder at the tricks of the trade.

A few years later I watched the building of the covered enclosures and I used to go in and drape myself over a barrier in the Jungle to watch the guys at work. I was not alone as lots of men, of a Celtic persuasion, used to wander in and we had some great blethers.

One old bloke was fascinating and he told us he had been the groundsman at Parkhead for 40 years. He was a quiet old Irish bloke and I was afraid to push him too hard in case he clammed up on his entertaining stories. He used to say he was only there to collect his pension and watch the grass growing, as well as keeping an eye on the groundstaff who had eventually taken over from him. The Irishman really was a bit of a quiet man but I remember him telling me he had been working as a labourer putting in the wooden steps on the terracing when the famous manager, Mr Willie Maley, came striding over and asked the contractor if 'his Irishman' could cut grass. He could, of course, and was hired to do that job. He said Mr Maley was a big, gruff but very fair man. I would love to have asked him how much he got paid but did not want to take advantage of his quiet, reserved nature.

But one day he surprised me, as we chatted, by asking if I knew that Celtic once had a horse. It was kept to pull the old roller and the machine which sowed the seeds and was allowed to graze on the park. The stable, he said, was behind the Rangers end of the ground and that, not only did they have a horse in those far-off days, they also had a van for the horse to pull and it was said to be a familiar sight in the east end as they made their way along the cobbled streets. Apparently the van carried the hampers with the strips to nearby away games, such as Clyde and Third Lanark.

It is all part of Celtic folklore and I heard it said that his pension was better than some people's wages but I have no complaint about that as I like to think of the faithful old servant being looked after in his old age.

James Canovan

THE game between Celtic and Atletico Madrid was a night to remember for all the wrong reasons. It was by far the worst night of football violence on the park I have ever witnessed in more than 50 years going to the game. Celtic players were punched, kicked and, even worse, spat on by the Spaniards. Jimmy Johnstone in particular came in for some very heavy treatment and I heard later he had to wash his hair at half time to get the disgusting spittle out of it. Those Madrid players were a disgrace to the sport and to their proud nation. And the only reason there wasn't a riot was that things got so bad the fans were almost in shock at the treatment handed out to the players.

Jimmy Brady, Coatbridge

I WAS put down, in the nicest possible way, at Parkhead more years ago than I care to remember – in the days when Friday was a day when fish, not meat, was on the menu. There I was, on a cold and bitter night, at a reserve game when our young boys boasted a team consisting of some of the finest talent in the country. We had laddies like Kenny Dalglish, Lou Macari, George Connelly, Davie Hay, Victor Davidson and others in our wee team and my own wee group was enjoying the match when half time came. Seeing an elderly man a few feet away, I asked him if he would like a Bovril, and he hit me with a one-liner Bob Hope would have been proud of: 'I never take meat on a Friday,' said he. Talk about red-faced!

Robert Arthur

The Night Tommy Gemmell
Blasted Benfica

MY memories of life at Parkhead span more than half a century and are a mixture of great excitement and marvellous humour, sprinkled with the occasional sadness. The excitement obviously concerns the great displays by Celtic, especially during the magnificent nine-in-a-row League campaign when Celtic's skill and entertainment value were unsurpassed. Who will ever forget the thrills of the big European nights when all the top teams from Italy, Spain, Holland and the rest of Europe came here on a regular basis? But Celtic under 'the Master', Jock Stein, always had an answer and it was unforgettable, and amazing to me, how our home-grown talent was able to match the best of the rest.

I'll never forget the explosive start to the match against Benfica in the European Cup in November 1969 when big Tommy Gemmell blasted home a free kick almost before we had time to realise the game had started. Willie Wallace and Harry Hood made it 3–0 that night and we thought we were home and dry. But Benfica had other things in mind and we went over there looking for a wee holiday only to get a rude awakening with a 3–0 defeat in Lisbon. But we got a wee rub of the green for once, when we went through on the toss of the coin. I was one of the estimated 80,000 who packed Parkhead for the first leg and was also in Lisbon for the return. And I'll never forget one of the saddest sights I've ever seen in football when the great Eusebio trudged past our supporters' bus carrying his boots in his hand and his face graphically told the story of his disappointment at going out that night.

That was the season Celtic went on to beat Fiorentina 3–1 on aggregate, Leeds United again 3–1 on aggregate, only to lose to Feyenoord in the final in Milan. The win over Don Revie's men is the stuff of which legends are made, but for me that night in Parkhead when we beat Benfica will live forever in my mind.

Don McGuinness, Dalmarnock

SO there we were in the Jungle discussing the speed merchants who had worn the hoops, and the names thrown up included, obviously, the Wee Buzz-Bomb himself, Bobby Lennox. Others worth a mention were Jimmy Quinn, who later moved to Clyde, and Stevie Chalmers. But a mate threw us all into disarray when he came up with someone called Billy – whose second name he couldn't remember. He was the fastest of them all, he said, and although he had never seen him play he had read all about him. We stood there wracking our brains for ages; it seemed as though the game would be finished before we found who this Billy guy was. You can imagine the scene as every Billy who had ever worn the jersey was trotted out. Mind you there weren't too many Billies. Suddenly my mate says he remembered who it was.

'It was Billy Whizz,' says he.

'Billy who?' says we.

'Billy Whizz, the guy from the children's comic,' he laughed before running for his life.

Joe Quigley, Tollcross

CELTIC were always to the forefront when 'firsts' were achieved, with the most notable being the first British club to win the European Cup in that never-to-be-forgotten night in Lisbon in 1967. And while they can't claim to be among the trend-setters when it came to installing floodlights, they can certainly point proudly to the fact that theirs were said to be the best of that era. I was there when Wolves, who were one of the really top English clubs at that time, came to Parkhead to hansel the lights. The pylons were 208 feet high and it was claimed they were the highest in the world. Anyway, when Wolves came up here in October 1959 there were about 45,000 supporters there to witness a wee bit of club history. We were not disappointed in the lights and I suppose it was a bit much to expect a young Celtic team to cope with the class and experience of Wolves. Unfortunately, the lights were so good we were spared nothing and saw Wolves prove they belonged to a higher grade than our lads. They won 2–0 with Broadbent and Murray scoring their goals and the Celtic team that night was John Fallon, Dunky MacKay, Neil Mochan, Eric Smith, Bobby Evans, Bertie Peacock, Steve Chalmers, Matt McVittie, Ian Lochhead, John Divers and Bertie Auld.

John Hanlon, Shettleston

THE vendor was making his way from the Celtic End into the Jungle with his tray of goodies when he tripped and lost his footing on the Jungle steps. His merchandise was scattered all over the place:

chewing-gum, Mars bars, the lot. The crowd waited to see what his reaction was going to be and minutes later fell about laughing. Dusting himself down, the super-smoothie salesman re-organised his cardboard boxes, replaced all his wares and, undaunted by his fall, shouted: 'Get your broken macaroon bars here . . .' That's style, that's the Jungle vendors.

Tom Lucas

The Day Charlie Tully Silenced the Fan

THIS memory of my experience of life in the Jungle remains vividly with me even though it happened many years ago. It concerned that great Irish international Charlie Tully, the supreme entertainer, who proved his wits were as fast as his twinkling feet in an incident I will never forget. As I was only a boy, I always took my place down at the front rows of the Jungle nearest the Celtic End. Charlie was nearing the end of his career in 1957 and Airdrie were the visitors to Parkhead, and the great man was being picked on by this one guy in the Jungle every time Charlie touched the ball. The fan was totally out of order and was being heckled and told to leave Charles Patrick alone. But he kept on going on at Charlie and when Tully won a corner at the Jungle side, the guy resumed his shouting. Charlie placed the ball at the corner flag and as he got ready to take the kick this guy shouted, 'Away Tully, ya mug ye, you're finished.' Charlie looked around and saw the man who was giving him the abuse. Quick as a flash, he walked over and held out his hand for the man to shake. The fan, abusive one minute, delighted to shake Charlie's hand the next, offered his hand in return. But Charlie was not daft. He took the man's hand and dragged him up on to the track and said for all to hear, 'You take it.' The heckler was shattered, Tully had won a landslide moral victory and the rest of the Jungle was delighted.

Kenny Hughes, Kings Park

CHAPTER SEVEN

Glen Daly's Fish-Supper Celebration

TERRY DICK'S recollections as he strolled down Memory Lane are worth a guinea an ounce. For those who don't know him, Terry is the son of that great Celtic character of yesteryear, singer-comedian Glen Daly, whose rendition of his very own 'Celtic Song' became a standard and all-time favourite with the Parkhead choir – especially those whose voices resounded around the Jungle terraces. Glen was one of the best known characters, if not *the* best known, who followed Celtic through six decades. His song became something of an anthem and sold more than a million copies worldwide. After retiring to Rothesay, Glen died a few years ago but his memory lives on in the hearts of Celtic fans and in the minds of his vast legion of fans who supported his regular concerts at the Ashfield Club in Glasgow where he became a legend. Terry is truly his father's son, with the same gift of the gab – as the following paragraphs reveal. He also has a voice to match his father's, god bless him.

Terry writes: 'Mum and Dad were both regular patrons of the Jungle around the late Thirties. They were courting at the time and Ella attended matches wearing her hat and gloves while the young Daly (Batholomew Dick) sported a hound's-tooth sports jacket, flannels, brogues and a white shirt with a big knot in the tie. If the action on the park became a bit heated and the crowd started swearing, Glen and Ella would move around a bit until they got a bit of peace.'

Terry recalls his father telling him of an incident in September 1938 when they were at their usual stance on the Jungle. 'A great Celtic side beat Rangers 6–2 and their joy was even more unrestrained when Ella revealed in Janefield Street, as they left the Jungle, that the Celts' victory had won her 12 shillings (60 pence) in the factory sweep. On the strength of her winnings the two of them spent the evening in the Orient picture-house in the Gallowgate; they also treated themselves to a celebratory fish supper, five Capstan cigarettes and a big bag of chocolate eclairs. My dad's wee brothers and sisters were not forgotten either as they got a "lucky tottie" each.' Paradise indeed.

His memory of his father's account was spot on, for the Celtic side that day was one of the most famous ever to wear the hoops: Kennaway, Hogg, Morrison, Geatons, Lyon, Paterson, Delaney, MacDonald, Crum, Divers, Murphy. Celtic's scorers that day were MacDonald (3), Delaney and Crum (2, one of them a penalty). A crowd of 74,500 crammed into Parkhead to watch that victory. Terry reveals his mother's favourite players were George Paterson – 'she loved how he parted his hair in the middle' – and 'a wee cheeky-looking guy called Johnny Crum, who looked as though he could have been a Chicago gangster'.

Glen's favourite was the hat-trick hero of that day, Malcolm MacDonald, who Glen often told his son was a wonderfully gifted and versatile player. 'My dad worshipped him and had followed his career ever since Malky had been a boy in the Garngad,' says Terry. He added, 'For as long as I can remember, even when the great Lisbon Lions team emerged, dad still maintained that MacDonald was the best ever.'

You can imagine Glen's joy when their paths crossed in the early Seventies on a tour of America. Terry explains: 'Dad always said he was fortunate indeed to spend a week with Malky in the New York/New Jersey area as a guest of the local Celtic Supporters Club.' Terry said: 'I'll never forget the effect that had on my dad. He was like a wee boy back rejoicing in the great days of the Jungle – a dream come true – to be your boyhood hero's pal. Dad said Malky, the man whose exploits he had cheered so long and so often from the Jungle, was such a gracious man and such a gentleman that after their meeting in America his status with my father was, if anything, even more enhanced. I think Malky must have spent most of that week telling dad of his playing career, not that he would need any encouragement, and their talks were repeated over and over to me many a time. When they were leaving at JFK airport, Malky held my sister's baby, Sean, in his arms and Daly was nearly greetin'. I think to him it was like a pilgrim handing a child to the Pope for a blessing. I'll never forget hearing that story and his words are etched in my brain – "Imagine Malky haudin' ma granwean!"' Until his death Glen maintained to Terry that his hero, Malcolm MacDonald, was not only the greatest but also the nicest guy ever to wear the hoops.

In later years Glen graduated to watching from the stand but he did not always have it so good according to Terry. Indeed, anything but.

Terry says: 'Round about 1928, as a wee boy from St Mary's Calton, the birthplace of the club, dad always felt an affinity with the team. As a youngster he was always a Jungle boy. However, because of hard times he invariably managed only the last 20 minutes of matches when the doors were opened and you got in for nothing. There was a ritual element involved. He would run up the Gallowgate, cut into Janefield Street, through the gate and into the heart of the Jungle at the centre line. After gathering himself he would launch into "Good Auld Celtic" and join enthusiastically in the singing of the supporters.

'He got another opportunity to sing solo, however, in 1961 when he recorded the Celtic Song. He was certainly proud of the association with the team but as the years passed he became terribly critical of the quality of the recording. Additionally, he felt that recording the song hadn't done him any favours in respect of mainstream Scottish show business. Certainly, the reaction in newspapers at the time – "controversial", "liable to cause trouble", "*that* song . . ." – suggests that in some quarters at least it was thought as being the wrong thing to do. However, John Murphy, a PE teacher friend of mine, started playing the record over the Parkhead sound system and almost from the word go the Jungle choir adopted it as their own very special anthem. Quite frankly the sound quality was so poor they could have been playing Dame Nellie Melba for all you heard of the lyrics and melody in the Jungle. I think Marconi himself installed the Jungle sound system.'

Terry jokes: 'Latterly dad used to say he wished they would stop playing the song, adding, "if they keep it up they'll put me in the grubber – anyway they still haven't paid me the six shillings and eight pence (34 pence) for the original copy".'

Seriously, though, Terry is rightly proud of his father and that song which everyone loved so well. And he says some of his proudest memories are the number of occasions he's stood at Parkhead and heard the massed choir, led by the Jungle of course, belting out 'Sure, it's a grand old team to play for . . .' Terry goes on: 'Hearing the fans in the Jungle, where my mother and father once stood, singing along with him on the record has a personal significance for my family. In the Centenary Year in 1988 my sister, Mary, came home from America – it was only a year after my father's death – and Celtic were about to clinch the Double. When Mary was here we went to one of the final League games with a large, buoyant crowd in attendance. Glen's record came on; he started singing and, as usual, the Jungle started giving it laldy; then gradually it was taken up all round the stadium, growing in intensity. Talk about goose bumps – and as you can appreciate Mary was in tears. It really was a very potent mixture of sorrow and pride.

It is certainly true that the lads in the Jungle love the players who wear the hoops, and always have done, but, equally, I am sure the players have a great deal of affection for the fans who stand on the terracing or now, regrettably, sit in the Jungle.'

IT is well known that the real characters, such as Jimmy Johnstone, Bertie Auld, wee Bobby Lennox and, from further back, Charlie Tully, loved hamming it up for the fans in the old 'cowshed'. Indeed, many years ago I remember reading in Charlie Tully's book how he loved to play for the Jungle Boys. The book was called *Passed to You* and the great and lovable Irishman, who gave us such joy and put the smile on the face of football, had some interesting things to say. It's worthwhile quoting from it, so here goes. Charlie wrote: 'The Parkhead terracing Tims know that if it's possible they can expect some clowning from me. They've been good to me, especially the boys in the Jungle, who travel home and away week in and winter out. I always try to please them for they are the real supporters of Celtic, the backbone you might say. A bit rough and ready, perhaps, and their language at times couldn't be called nice, but these boys know their football. And, of this much you can be certain, if I didn't produce the goods on the field, if I didn't measure up to some of the players they've been used to in the past, they wouldn't tolerate me for a minute. Do I play to the gallery? You're darned tootin'!'

Peter McBride, Bothwell

Wartime Memories

MY first experience of being in the Jungle occurred during the war and I can't remember the date, but it followed soon after George Paterson had bounced the ball past 'Cowboy' Jenkins to give Celtic a 1–0 win over Rangers.

I recall that game in particular as it was the first time I had gone to Celtic Park and, in my ignorance, complete with my Rangers scarf I had gone into the home end. That I was able to enjoy the game was due to a group of elderly Celtic supporters whose protection I enjoyed until they put me on a tramcar to Partick.

I had moved into the centre of the Jungle for my next visit, the dividing line between the Old Firm diehards, and the repartee was priceless. It was an invigorating experience for a youngster like myself. Suddenly, from the Celtic end of the Jungle, the police pulled a young soldier. He had obviously been imbibing well, if not wisely. This was in the days when one could go to a match with a 'good bead on' and still be admitted. The tussle on the pitch became secondary as the crowd, to a man, berated the upholders of the law as only a Glasgow crowd can do. The policemen's antecedents were of questionable morality and their destination in the afterworld was assured. I will never forget the picture of this Glasgow copper during a bitter Old Firm match, as he walked the unfortunate soldier, complete with his green-and-white scarf, protesting, 'We're no liftin' him, honest, we're just putting him ootside in case he gets hurt.' For some reason, which I do not understand even now after all these years, the officers walked the alcoholically impaired soldier right round the Rangers end of the ground subjected to such a torrent of abuse as would scorch the hide off an elephant.

I also remember when the Scottish League Select took 11 goals off the Irish League and the residents of the Jungle gave big Ian Ure, of Dundee, a terrible time because he had replaced their favourite, Billy McNeill. In the past, as a neutral, I have found the Jungle an entertaining place to watch the game but I must regret having to forego the pleasure of enjoying the repartee of the rational Celtic supporters because of a bigoted minority which the club's management do nothing to deter.

Gilbert Falconer, Kelvindale

Packie's Proudest Moment

IT goes without saying that one of the proudest days in my career with Celtic was my testimonial match against a Republic of Ireland Select side at Parkhead on 12 May 1991. It never crossed my mind when I came here as a young lad from Donegal in 1978 that I would be honoured in this way and when it happened I was overwhelmed. To see all my family around me on that great occasion and then watch my Celtic team-mates and my international colleagues line up to honour me was an unforgettable feeling and one that I will forever cherish.

But another aspect of that great day was that it gave me an opportunity to pay tribute to the fans in the Jungle as it's not often a goalkeeper gets the chance to go across to that part of the ground to salute the fans. Keepers are usually kept well away from that area as we normally just run to one end or the other. This time I took great pleasure from being able to run right up to them to show them my delight, not only at being there that day, but for the fantastic support they had given me during my entire career with Celtic.

The fans who occupied the Jungle really are exceptional. With respect to all our fans and to other areas in the park, the Jungle fans have always been acknowledged as the leaders of the pack – the trendsetters if you like. It was always from that area the singing started and swept round the stadium. They were the ones who had the power to raise you when things were not going so well. I am certain they won an awful lot of games for us when they got behind the team and literally lifted them to victory by the volume of their backing. We have enjoyed some wonderful backing over the years in domestic games, at League and Cup level. And the European nights have been truly fantastic occasions.

But I have to be a wee bit selfish here and say that my testimonial match was something really special and to see so many of my international pals turning up for me was something that will live with me forever.

The Celtic line-up for that game was: Bonner, Wdowczyk, Rogan, Grant, Elliott, Whyte, Creaney, Galloway, Coyne, Nicholas Fulton. The substitutes were Baillie, McNally, Dziekanowski, Miller and Walker. The Republic Select were Peyton, Hughton, Staunton, Stapleton, Moran, Houghton, Slaven, Townsend, Quinn, Kelly,

Sheedy. On the bench were O'Brien, Aitken, my twin brother, Denis, and Liam Brady.

Pat Bonner

A CROWD of 70,000 were at Celtic Park to witness Charlie Tully's first big game, a League Cup clash with Rangers. The Ibrox men's Iron Curtain defence of Young, Cox and Shaw were visibly shell-shocked at the end of a Tully-inspired drubbing which ended up 3–1 but might well have been six or seven. The Rangers defenders simply could not handle this boy, whose flicks, crosses and dummies were something that very few of the vast crowd had ever seen.

The support loved him; there was a combination of the talent of a Patsy Gallagher and the comedy of a Tommy McInally. A supporters' song of that era, to the tune of 'How Can You Buy Killarney?', went like this: 'How can you buy all the cups that he's won? How can you buy old Ma Tully's son? How can you purchase that son of a gun: How can you buy our Charlie?'

Celtic Programme, 20 April 1993

MONDAY, 28 August 1899 attracted 12,000 people to Celtic Park for Sandy McMahon's benefit match against Rangers. The Duke himself did not play after taking a knock at Rugby Park on Saturday. Rangers regular keeper Matt Dickie took a fall from the Ibrox brake (bus) outside the ground, which meant that Willie Howden, a junior (who incidentally played the odd game for Celtic), was drafted in as deputy. Jet-haired Pat Gilhooly, the darling of the fans, put Celtic ahead in 17 minutes but Bob Hamilton equalised. The second half lasted only 30 minutes as darkness closed in. Celtic did experiment in their early years with floodlighting but scrapped them in 1894. Flying winger Jack Bell – the *Evening Times* brought out a special edition when Celtic splashed out £300 on his transfer in 1896 – put Celtic back in front, but Hamilton was equal to anything Celtic might do and equalised again and the game ended 2–2. And by the end of the night The Duke was £400 richer.

Celtic signed him from Hibernian after paying him double his Easter Road wages, but during pre-season training in 1892 Nottingham Forest waved a bag of sovereigns (literally) under the young Duke's nose and he fled south. In no time Celtic were on the trail, John Glass, Mick Dunbar, Davie Meikleham and the Duke's own brother in pursuit at various stages. Davie Meikleham even

101

shaved his beard to walk the streets of Nottingham incognito. The telegraph wires hummed hot between Parkhead and the Trent and Sandy eventually came back to Glasgow on 23 August 1892, fed up with skulking in Sherwood Forest hamlets and London hotels, to dedicate the next ten years to Celtic. He probably ranks as the first Celt with whom an era of the club's history can be identified.

He ran a pub, the Duke's Bar in Great Eastern Street, and died during the close season of 1916, aged about 44.

Celtic Programme, 27 August 1991

OUT of Celtic's 66 European ties they have lost the first leg on 16 occasions. But of these 16 occasions they have still managed to go through eight times, a 50 per cent success rate.

Celtic Programme, 6 November 1991

I NOW know for sure that I am not the only one who misses not only the Jungle but all the other standing enclosures around the country.

For years my pal and I went to our own regular spot in the Jungle and enjoyed every minute of the banter and close companionship we picked up in there every other week for many years. Now it's all gone and, honestly, I'll never feel the same. I'll not make the mistake of saying something like 'I'll not be back', for I could never stay away for any length of time, but I'll admit it won't be the same from now on after the closure of the Jungle.

And I'm not alone, for a friend showed me an article in the Motherwell FC programme which was on about this thorny subject of all-seated stadia. It was telling the fans that the St Johnstone game on 14 May 1994 would be the last occasion when fans could stand on the terracing at Fir Park as after that it would be all-seated on four sides. I got the article from him to show that it is not only Celtic fans who like to stand – as it applies to supporters from other clubs as well. It says:

'We all have fond memories of standing at a crush barrier enjoying a football match and, to be fair, there was also a downside to viewing from an open terracing. A sudden downpour or a sudden fall of snow would quickly transform this scenario into a bit of miserable experience – particularly if your team finished up on the losing side, soaked to the skin and feeling really miserable. Despite this, for generations, football fans turned out in their thousands. In the past they were more discriminating than the modern fans who seem to go to matches because the facilities are good. Quality football often comes a poor second to comfort plus a winning team – irrespective of how the final result is achieved.

'One great point about the terracings – if you didn't like the company you had landed among then you simply moved along until you were happier with your new group of fans. In a grandstand if you land beside an obnoxious individual you are stuck with him for 90 minutes (or the whole season if you are a season-ticket holder). I know of one old fan who has stood on the north terracing since the war. He will not be back next season because he does not enjoy watching a game while he is seated – "Ach I'll go and see the Hamilton Accies or somebody else," he told me. Yes, old habits die hard.

'Taking the broad view, all-seated stadia are a vast improvement, but a small reserved area for standing supporters would not go amiss.'

Tony Gallagher, Motherwell

YOU'VE all heard I am sure the great cry, 'There's the last of the milk chocolate and spearmint chewing-gum'. It's always the *last* you will notice, although the vendor may have a barrowload of the stuff outside waiting for supplies to run out. This day, however, it was lashing down with rain and one of the sellers was meandering through the Jungle making very few sales of his wares. Despite his well-rehearsed script and merit award from the Carnegie Foundation of Sales Management, things were not going well. His cry could be heard drifting over the heads of the crowds but it was all to no avail. He was stuck with his chewing-gum and he knew it. His sales pitch was falling on deaf ears although, to be fair to him, he kept on with the monotonous chant. Finally, though, enough was enough even for this super salesman. Putting down his tray, he shouted as loudly as he could, 'Is there naebody gonnae buy any of this effing chocolate and spearmint chewing-gum 'cos I'm bloody soaking through and frozen cauld?'

That did it: within seconds of his impassioned plea the guy was descended on by about 20 fans who bought out his entire stock.

Joe Bradley, Coatbridge

PLEASE spare my blushes and just call me Jimmy while I tell you the tale of how I almost got my ticket punched, quite literally, on the train.

My mate and I were going to a midweek game between Falkirk and Celtic at Brockville more years ago than I care to remember. But it was so long ago the trains were leaving from the old Buchanan Street station in Glasgow, so that will give you a clue. Being good regular Jungle boys we had managed to get ourselves tickets, which were like gold dust. Or, to be strictly accurate, I had managed to get us two tickets.

We had arranged to meet at the corner of Parliamentary Road and Buchanan Street and I was there early, champing at the bit and raring to get to Brockville. Needless to say, my pal was late. I wondered what the devil had happened to him and decided to give him until five minutes before the train was due to leave. I thought, well, he'd do the same for me, but as time wore on I was getting more annoyed with him and anxious that I would miss the kick-off. I was also now convinced he was not going to arrive.

Then, just when I saw the guard nipping out of his van, a Celtic fan came running up the station platform shouting, 'Anybody got any spare tickets for the gemme?' He had obviously been running for miles to get there so, with an eye on the clock and my pal's time being just about up, I took pity on the poor soul and gave him my mate's ticket. I don't have to tell you the rest. Yes, you're right, You've guessed it. As the guard raised his green flag and put the whistle up to his lips I heard my pal's voice shouting, 'Haud the train.'

I turned round and there he was, nearly blue in the face and that must have been hard enough for him to bear, as he gasped out what could have been his last words,' Jings, I almost didnae make it.'

To which I replied, 'Jings, and I've gone and sold your ticket.'

Jimmy

HERE'S how I felt about the old Jungle where I watched my heroes, man and boy, for 40-odd years:

> We waited
> and we waited
> Thirty minutes before it began
> The crowd grew bigger
> and bigger
> The sky was crystal clear
> The air filled with tension
> No one moved,
> no one stirred
> Silent and motionless
> Waiting for the time

Idle chat, running humour,
'Is that not?', 'It cannot be?', But it was
And the appointed time came.
The noise rose, like Phoenix from the ashes
Crowds shunted and waved,
Banners, flags, caps, hurled into the sky
A crescendo erupted
And from the Jungle we could see
Small running figures and a voice cried out
'Aw naw, it's only the ball boys again.'

Tom Lucas

HERE is one Jungle recollection that demands inclusion – simply because of the honesty and bold approach of the writer:

'I am probably an unexpected source of information for the history of the Jungle. I am a Hun, yes a Blue Nose. Let me explain. In the early Seventies at Old Firm games there was segregation but Rangers fans were allowed almost, but not quite, up to the halfway line in the Jungle. This particular memory is of a game on 12 September 1970 and concerns the referee for the match, one Bill Mullan of Dalkeith in Midlothian. At that time I attended Lasswade High School, the local 'proddie' school and Mr Mullan was head PE teacher at Dalkeith's St David's. We know Rangers fans' reaction to referees, 'who's the Fenian in the black?' etc. Well, on this occasion they were right as far as myself and my friend were concerned.

'As is the case in most Old Firm games, there was a controversial incident when Colin Stein, the Rangers No. 9, ran from about the halfway line and put the ball in the net only to look round and see Bill Mullan had stopped play for offside. Nothing unusual in that you may think, but it appeared to me Mr Mullan was laughing his socks off. I was not quite at the point of invading the pitch, but it's fair to say I was livid, eyes bulging and shouting all sorts of abuse. My feeling, right there and then, was of going down to Dalkeith the following Saturday morning, where Mr Mullan refereed school games, and of 'punching his lights out.

'Thankfully, when the time came round I had cooled down and can now laugh at the incident. There was at least a happy ending for the Celtic fans, if not for me – their team won 2–0 with goals from Hughes and Murdoch.'

Alan Jones, Lasswade

CHAPTER EIGHT

Only an Excuse – For a Laugh

RANGERS were not the last team to win a trophy and parade it in front of the Jungle. That is a cast-iron fact and I have it from no less an authority than that very fine actor, scriptwriter and lifelong Celtic fan Tony Roper. And he should know – for he was the winning captain. It was he who was carried shoulder high in triumph before his adoring fans and the man who has had us all in stitches for years loved every minute of it. It came on the 'Blow away the Blues' night when almost 20,000 fans turned up to say farewell to two institutions: the Lisbon Lions and the Jungle. The fact Tony was there was 'only an excuse' to join the fun and celebrations that night of 1 June 1993.

Tony explains: 'We were all there to join in the festivities and it was a fabulous night. I was there in my playing capacity, of course, as one of the world-famous Dukla Pumpherston team of superstars. But, to be honest, I was also there to say cheerio to the Lions in their testimonial year and to be part of the nostalgia of the last game before the Jungle was all seated. It was a marvellous night all round. The Lions were magic, with wee Jimmy Johnstone needing a ball of his own as he ran rings round the Manchester United lads *and* his own team-mates at times. The fans in the Jungle were unbelievable in their support for absolutely everyone who was there – no matter who they were. It mattered not a jot to them if they were Celtic players, United men, musicians, singers or even the megastars of Dukla Pumpherston. Whoever was there was cheered to the echo. It was that kind of night. Everything that moved was cheered, and I can tell you the fans were not the only ones who loved every second of it. We all did – especially me.

'For I have a story to tell that changes football history. Rangers are not the last team to win a trophy on the hallowed turf of Parkhead before the Jungle – they may have thought they were when they beat Aberdeen a couple of weeks before to take the Scottish Cup and the Ibrox punters were obviously delighted at the thought of being the last winners there. But they had reckoned without the boys of DP – Dukla Pumpherston is our name and football is our game. We beat the stars of *Coronation Street* and at the end of it all I thought that was it. I was wrong. There was a cup at stake and Danny McGrain told me to go up and get it and show it off to the packed Jungle

'"Me?" says I.

'"You," says he.

'And no matter how much I pleaded with Danny to go and get it he was having none of it. It was up to me to get the cup and show it to the fans. Proud? I was chuffed to bits. And I did it wearing the right colours, too, for although it was the lads from *Coronation Street* who wore the green and white hoops, yer man had on his very own Celtic top under my Whitecraigs Suzuki sponsored shirt. There was no way I was going to fulfil my lifelong dream of playing at Parkhead and not wear the hoops. They were on, but tucked under my other top. But when Danny ordered me to get the trophy and take it to the Jungle, off came the top. There I was in all my glory in my Celtic top and right proud of it I was too. What a reception we got. The fans loved it as we hammed it up with me being carried high and guys like big Gerry Collins, Brian McLaughlin and the rest of the lads joining in the fun. Magic. And I'll never forget it.

'The *Celtic View* photographer had a field day as the lads carried me around showing off that cup. Now I don't want it to sound as though I was going overboard about that night but, see that picture – I've had it framed; I've had it made into coasters; and if I could think of anything else to do with the picture, I would do it. We even got a medal as a memento of that night and it's sitting there in pride of place in my display cabinet. What a night, what memories!

'I'd been to the Jungle many times before although I've got to say I was in the main a Celtic End man. But I've been back to the Jungle since that big night – only this time it's a shade more genteel with seats and all but it's a rare view and still a fine place to watch the match from. I still go back and every time I do I think of that great cup-winning night and of me being carried shoulder high. **Magic!** I'm one of those people who think that progress has been made and that football should be watched from a seat. But I'll tell you something, it doesn't stop me leaping to my feet when I've got something to shout about. The days of the Kop and the Jungle may have gone, but they have left us with a million good memories.'

CRANNIE was a character. I never ever met him but I never tired of hearing stories from older relations about him; some of them I am sure were apocryphal.

It was said about Crannie that the nearest he could have got to heaven was to stand in the Jungle at his beloved Paradise. He would happily have pitched his tent in the old, dilapidated cowshed and, when it was refurbished with new roof and concrete steps, Crannie would have felt it akin to living in a five-star hotel.

Legend has it that Crannie's devotion to the Bhoys had reached such a quality of selflessness that the board decided on a course of action never taken before or since: they actually allowed Crannie to run up and down the track behind the linesman – and that was in the days of the great Jimmy Delaney, who was a real wizard of the wing. Crannie always chose to be on Jimmy's side of the park, even if it meant leaving his beloved Jungle steps, and whenever Jimmy picked up the ball to go haring down the wing and cross one of those perfectly delivered hanging balls, Crannie was off down the track after him. It was as though he was Delaney's shadow.

But, one very wet and windy day, Delaney had got the ball and set off at lightning speed down the wing. Crannie went after him as usual, but this time it went wrong. Crannie slipped and fell, sprawling face down in the track! But, undeterred, he raised his head and shouted at the top of his voice: 'Carry on Jimmy, don't wait for me.'

Wee Bob, Easterhouse

I HAVE very many marvellous memories of Celtic winning at home and abroad, but one match that gives me a sour taste every time I even think about it is the meeting with Rapid Vienna at Parkhead in November 1984.

There is absolutely no doubt in my mind that defeat not only cost the club about £1m that season, but it also set us back for years as we were in the ascendancy at the time and a good Cup run would have generated much more revenue for the club.

Things had been looking good when we went into that European Cup Winners Cup tie with the Austrians at Parkhead for, although we were 3–1 down from the first leg, we knew we were more than capable of pulling that back at home. We did, as we eventually won 3–0, with great goals by Brian McClair, Murdo MacLeod, and Tommy Burns, but the Austrians got away with murder.

One of their guys fell to the ground claiming he had been struck by a bottle thrown from the Jungle. But, miraculously, there was no mark on the player. Anyway, there was an inquiry and UEFA fined both clubs and ordered a third game to be played more than 200 miles away. It took place at Old Trafford and we lost 1–0 to go out on aggregate, but I will never change my point of view that Celtic were cheated out of that tie. It was a diabolical disgrace that Rapid were allowed to get away with it and I feel certain that if we had gone through we would have gone on to win the Cup that season.

So, although I have very many happy memories of the Jungle it is that horrible one that comes to mind and, sadly, I don't think I'll ever be able to forget it.

Ricky Fearon, Celtic Supporters Club

Pat Woods – an Authority on the Bhoys

PAT WOODS never had the good fortune to pull on a Celtic jersey so he set about doing the next best thing – following the team and writing about their glorious history. And the man, who earns his living as a librarian only a long free kick from Parkhead, is acknowledged as arguably the best historian of the fortunes of Celtic Football Club – which is hardly surprising, I suppose, when you consider he could rattle off the names of all the award-winning teams before he was old enough to go to school.

Books are not only his livelihood, they are his hobby, so it followed that if he was going to write he should write about his beloved Celtic. And he has done so with great success, along with fellow authors Tom Campbell and Kevin McCarra. *The Glory and the Dream*, by Pat and Tom, is a marvellous read and *Rhapsody in Green* is a testimony to their knowledge of the club, its players and its supporters.

Pat was eager to jot down his memories of his time spent in the Jungle at Parkhead, starting from his days when he was carried there on the shoulders of his father. As we chatted during my research, Pat recalled: 'It all started for me, I suppose, in the early Fifties when I was a wee boy and saw my first Celtic game. At that time Celtic had great players of ability and personality, such as John McPhail and Charlie Tully. My early days were inspired by my father, James Woods, who never tired of telling me of the ability of Patsy Gallacher. I used to sit at his knee, entranced by his stories – one in particular, the 1931 Scottish Cup final. The way my father told it was great, it was just like being there. He told me of the newspaper that had to be recalled as it had the wrong scoreline caused by a late equaliser by Celtic. The paper had started printing the story that Motherwell had beaten Celtic 2–1 to win the Cup. But it had to be recalled as Celtic drew level at 2–2. Celtic then won the replay with Jimmy McGrory and Bertie Thomson scoring two apiece. Now I had heard all this at my father's knee but when I started researching for *Rhapsody in Green* I found his memory had been almost photographic – it was astonishing how accurate his recollections had been. I used to remember all these stories off by heart almost and at New Year, when relatives came, I was trotted out to do my party piece and recite the great Celtic teams of the past.

'I suppose I was a studious child and it came easy to me. That was how I became interested in books and history. It was some time, though, before my pleading to be taken to see Celtic finally paid off and it only did as I think my father was tired of listening to me moaning every week about not seeing the team I had heard so much about. When he finally relented I was up early on a Saturday, ready to go almost after breakfast. We travelled to Parkhead on a No. 23 tram which came from Baillieston, passed through Shettleston, where I stayed, and on to Parkhead. The trams were always packed and we normally had to stand, but I never complained. My father bought me sweets and the thought of going to the Jungle kept me going. I'll never forget the sights that awaited you each week. I was lucky as my father always lifted me over the turnstiles, but there were scores of wee boys, all of them pleading to be lifted over and to get in for nothing.

'I always remember the men who busked outside for pennies. They played the accordion or mouth organ while going round with the bunnet. Then we would get in and I never ever lost my excitement. The Jungle was the place to be as, apart from the grandstand on the other side, it was the only place with cover if it rained. And it usually did. It was not until 1957 that the Celtic End was covered and the Rangers End followed 11 years later. Anyway, we all huddled together and it was great being a boy then. There were always plenty of witty people in the Jungle and it was part of my education, I suppose, listening to their patter. I remember all the talk about the Jungle fans being too partisan and it also had a reputation for having nothing but really tough guys in there. It was all a bit of a myth and I never saw any trouble and always enjoyed my time spent in there. My father used to have to lift me up on his shoulders to see the game and there was never a complaint. Wee boys got away with a lot, I suppose, and I was a wee smout.

'In those early days it was only an earth terracing and the smart Jungle regulars knew where to stand. They searched around to see where the rain patches were on the earth and avoided them as they knew there must be a leak in the corrugated-iron roof above that spot. But, again, there were few complaints as it was better than standing out in the elements all the time.

'My hero at that time was Bobby Evans, I thought he was terrific then and still do. He was perpetual motion and nobody worked harder for a Celtic win than Bobby. My father couldn't see beyond Charlie Tully. He was his big favourite and we used to argue on the way home about who had the better game. It was all great fun and I loved that part of my time as a Celtic fan. I used to be so excited that when I went home I would go out to play football with my pals and I always had to pretend to be Bobby Evans.

'I remember the wee boys who used to come into the Jungle as we were going out. When I first saw them I wondered why they had big sacks and bags with them. I soon found out it was for the empty beer bottles which they took to the family department of the pubs to get money back for them.

'One thing about going to the Jungle that sticks out in my mind was a call I used to hear which does not happen now. I recall hearing it around the early Sixties and this man near me was shouting, "Come on the Sons of Dan." I hadn't a clue what that meant and when I asked him he gave me a history lesson. It was all about Celtic's Irish connections and the patriot Daniel O'Connell.

'Another occasion locked into my brain was the sight of Jock

Stein coming out one day before a game and looking all around the stadium. He glanced, in particular, at the packed Jungle and rubbed his hands as if to say, "We'll get plenty of support from in there today." As usual, the Big Man was right.

'In my later years supporting Celtic from the Jungle I was almost in awe as I looked around me at the fanaticism of the fans. It almost took on a life of its own during the big games and Jock Stein was right when he said the fans were like an extra man. I recall the European tie with St Etienne in particular, when the fans roared Celtic back from 2–0 down over there to a 4–2 aggregate win here. The French manager, Herbin, wrote later in his autobiography that the Celtic fans had influenced the referee. I bought his book in France and can recall him writing that the fans in the Jungle behaved like ancient Roman spectators in the Colosseum – it was almost as though they were looking for a fight to the death. I was in the Jungle that night we beat St Etienne and it was unforgettable. I was right in the middle and those of us there knew before the rest when the teams were ready to come out. The photographers used to huddle down in front of the tunnel and when they got up and started walking backwards you knew it was time for the fun to start. The cheering started in that centre spot of the Jungle and was carried on in a wave all around the ground. It was a Mexican wave of noise long before that kind of support was ever heard of.

'That game was one of my great memories but I have very many more, such as the win over Liverpool and the other great European nights. On those occasions the Jungle was always the place that filled up first. They loved the gallus characters such as Bertie Auld and the wee man Jimmy Johnstone could do no wrong for them. On the other hand, if big John Hughes had an off-day, the fans were merciless – which I think was a shame as big Yogi was a great player for Celtic. He tried his hardest in every single match he played and gave us some great times. To me, Yogi was a great sight in full flow and I'll never forget him and I thank him for my memories.

'Now the seats are in and the atmosphere has changed. But then so, too, has football in general. Gone are the days of the cloth-cap image and they have been replaced with big business and football is now a money-making industry. But I am certain that if the Jungle was ever re-opened as a standing area it would be the first place in the ground to fill up once more . . . And I would be among the first in the queue to rekindle old memories.'

LOU MACARI was one of a wave of players who came to Celtic just behind the team which won the European Cup in Lisbon in 1967. Others who came around then included Kenny Dalglish and Lou teamed up with Kenny quite a lot then. He made his name with United basically as a midfield man, but when he first burst on to the Celtic scene it was as a striker. As a youngster he had the same scoring knack as Jimmy Greaves. That's who he reminded me of. Lou would be in that box snapping up the crumbs and scoring regularly.

Jock Stein, *Lou Macari Testimonial Programme*

LIVING in England can have some compensations – let's face it, it has to have some compensations going for it, especially for a Scot who is a Celtic fan. Anyway, my compensation has been that, although I get home regularly for matches at Parkhead, I have been lucky to be almost on the doorstep when Celtic come down here regularly for testimonial matches. The club has always been in demand for these games for everyone knows Celtic always make them challenge games and not merely friendlies.

Among the ones I have been lucky to see were those for Bobby Moore at West Ham, Ron Yeats at Liverpool, Jack Charlton at Leeds, David O'Leary at Arsenal, and, of course, Lou Macari at Manchester United. There have been many more over the years but I've missed some of them. All were great occasions and my workmates couldn't believe so many would have made the journey to pay tribute to players who had no connection with Celtic. It was different in the case of Macari as he had been a Celt but, even then, the attendance at Old Trafford was half Celtic and the other half Manchester United. And we all had a great time.

Fred Mitchell, Manchester

CELTIC FOOTBALL AND ATHLETIC CLUB LTD, founded 1888, revolutionised 1994.

Once a Tim Special, March 1994

A 'Billy Connolly Tale' that Really Happened

BILLY CONNOLLY got hold of this story and told it as only he can, but believe me it actually happened to me in the Sixties in the Jungle. At half time during a Celtic *v* Dunfermline match I retired to the toilet and there were only two of us there. The other gentleman, pie in hand while doing the necessary with the other, amiably remarked to me, 'I wonder how the animals are getting on?' That's the truth. Honest.

Sorry to have to repeat this but my other memory also concerns a similar human function. My friend and I were again in the Jungle when we suddenly felt a warm sensation at the rear of our trousers. Sure enough, you can guess the rest. I turned to remonstrate with the culprit, pointing to the close proximity of the toilet. I was immediately met with the rejoinder, 'You should be in the Stand with the rest of the f...... snobs.' I continued to try to point out that his behaviour was rather unsociable but I was finally silenced by his withering aside to his pal: 'This is the kind of b...... that shows his wife his pay packet.' It is true, of course.

Neil McDermott

IT'S not very often a team can give Rangers a goal of a start in the first minute, still be trailing at half time, and end up winning 5–1. But it happened in January 1966 and I am glad to say I was there to witness it.

It was Davy Wilson who gave Rangers the lead after just 90 seconds and the Jungle was quiet and it stayed that way until just after half time. Then it burst into life when Steve Chalmers equalised. It was to turn out to be a fantastic performance from Stevie as that was the first of a glorious hat-trick. Joe McBride executed the perfect dummy as Tommy Gemmell swung the ball into goal and Chalmers raced in to hammer the ball past Billy Ritchie. Stevie then put Celtic in front, heading in one of Charlie Gallagher's accurate corners, and Gallagher himself and Bobby Murdoch made it 4–1 before Chalmers finished off an astonishing comeback in great style after Jimmy Johnstone's shot had come back off a post in the last minute.

That was the real never-say-die spirit we always associated with Celtic teams but, sadly, that ingredient was the thing that was missing as Celtic struggled to combat Rangers' supremacy in the early Nineties. We will only ever regain our rightful place when we rediscover that will to win.

Tony McIntyre, Maryhill

BILLY MCNEILL will forever be associated with the No. 5 strip at Parkhead but I can remember him from the start of his career when he lined up at right-back with Bobby Evans at centre-half. Sometimes he even lined up at right-half alongside Evans and Bertie Peacock, but for me it was all immaterial as Billy went on to prove himself No. 1 at Parkhead.

Harry Martin

MANY years ago my son, Anthony, who is now aged 35 and living in Australia, was in the Jungle for a game against Rangers. I suppose he would be about 12 at the time and he had taken with him a marvellous and highly unusual Celtic tea-towel. It was very decorative and all about Celtic's great victory in Lisbon in 1967. I'd never seen anything like it before or since.

My boy was very proud of it, since it appeared he was the only one who had it. And when Celtic scored in that match he waved it above his head and a passing policeman grabbed it and took it off him. When he came home and told me about this I wrote to the Chief Constable, complaining about the incident. I was told to go to the Tobago Street HQ and look through the bags which were full of flags that had been confiscated. My wife and I both went there and, after searching through hundreds of Celtic flags, banners, etc., we failed to find it. My lad was upset but later a police inspector came to my house with the towel and apologised, saying the policeman who had taken it from my boy was a greenhorn from the country.

Some years later we met an American Celtic fan after a game in Aberdeen and I gave him the tea-towel as a souvenir.

G. Quinn, Springburn

The Jungle and the Kop – Shankly

THE atmosphere at Celtic Park, with its famous Jungle, and Anfield, the home of Liverpool with its equally renowned Kop, are almost identical. And that is official, for it came from no less a person than Bill Shankly, who was so close to his friend and confidante Jock Stein.

Shanks wrote his name into the books of great football quotations when he burst into the dressing-room in Lisbon in 1967, minutes after Celtic had won the European Cup, to hug his great pal Jock and say: 'John, you're immortal.'

Bill made his feelings known on the similarity between the Jungle and the Kop during a visit to Parkhead in August 1973, when Stein's men played a friendly match with Penarol, of Uruguay, and Celtic chairman Desmond White made a presentation of a beautiful clock to Shanks. The normally irrepressible Shankly was rendered almost speechless, but he recovered to say later how proud he had been to receive the presentation from a club he had always admired.

He told the *Celtic View*: 'It was a magnificent gesture by Celtic to even consider making a presentation to me and as for the Celtic fans, their reception gave me an even greater thrill if that was possible. It's the men who stand on the terracings and sit in the stands who make professional football possible and their welcome for me was out of this world.'

He added: 'In my early days Celtic and Rangers were the ultimate in football and, since my playing career was spent in England, I couldn't have imagined that one day I would stand in the middle of Celtic Park and be given a reception like the one I received. To be honest, I was very nervous and excited before the presentation, and even a little overawed out there, but during the ceremony I heard the crowd and felt so much at home it was like standing in the middle of the Kop at Anfield.'

Celtic View, 8 August 1973

THE spontaneous wit of the Jungle fans was never more clearly illustrated than on the night of Jimmy Johnstone and Bobby Lennox's joint testimonial. Big Billy Connolly was the referee for an 'Old

Crocks'-style match on that great night. And the Big Yin decided to have a wee bit of fun at the expense of his wee pal, Jimmy. He ran out on to the park wearing a Rangers scarf just to wind-up the wee man but the Jungle spotted it right away and started giving the bird. Big Billy responded by producing a red card and sending the entire Jungle off. But, quick as a flash and as though it had been rehearsed, the Jungle to a man shouted: 'You can stick your yellow wellies up your a..., you can stick your yellow wellies up your a..., you can stick your yellow wellies, stick your yellow wellies, stick your yellow wellies up your a...'. In fairness, the big man took it brilliantly and joined in the fun.

Tommy McKenna, Coatbridge

SINCE Denis Connaghan played in goal against Dundee United in the 1974 Scottish Cup final, Celtic have played in eight Cup finals without a Scottish-born goalkeeper.

Celtic Programme, 22 January 1994

Jungle Fans Are Special – Roy Aitken

I THINK if you asked any Celtic player about the Jungle they would tell you it was really special. And I am no different, but what I will say is that I think it would be unfair just to single out those fans in there. To me, all Celtic fans were special people.

In reality, all supporters who followed Celtic were, to me, and all the other players, special for they never gave us anything other than loyal and total support.

But what I have to say about the Jungle is that most of the songs and cheers began there and I think that is where the most fervent and committed Celtic fans stood. You were always guaranteed that part of the ground would be packed out for every game and I think that's why the Jungle picked up the reputation it had over the years. It always looked a formidable sight when you ran out. The colours and the noise just hit you straight in the face. It was awesome.

Tales of the Jungle had obviously done the rounds, with its reputation going before it. Some of our players who had gone south had obviously done a bit of talking about it and when other players joined us in later years they seemed to know all about it. I don't know what they had been told, but one or two seemed a wee bit taken aback and almost stunned by the sight of it when they were confronted by the empty space. One guy even said to me, as we walked out over the park: 'Is that it?' But when it came time for him to run out to face it on his first game at Celtic Park he quickly changed his mind.

Memories of my 15 years of playing in front of the Jungle remain vivid in my mind. There are certain games that stick out, well apart from the others. The day we won the Premier League Championship as the first half of the Centenary Double in 1988 was incredible. The ground was chock-a-block, the Jungle was awash with people and it just burst into life when we ran out. Another happy occasion was my testimonial game against Manchester United and, of course, all the big European nights were fantastic.

It also goes without saying that all the Old Firm games were special occasions and although the Jungle has now gone as such, it will still have its own unique atmosphere for it will still be the area nearest to the pitch, and the players and fans both take something from that closeness. But it also has its own tradition, with fathers taking their children there and even now it is seated that may still happen there.

But, for me, the Jungle will still be the Jungle, whether people are standing or sitting.

Roy Aitken

SOME players, because of their outgoing characters as much as their ability, made their mark on the fans in the Jungle. But one man I will always admire was Tom McAdam, who was so often the unsung hero for Celtic. Tom showed his versatility and skill when Billy McNeill converted him from a forward to a central defender, but he showed he had lost none of his striking ability by scoring eight goals against Rangers. He was always a favourite of the Jungle for his wholehearted play, but these goals merely cemented his relationship with the fans, who just loved putting it over on their old rivals. One of his finest games against Rangers was in September 1978 when I remember him scoring twice in a 3–1 win at Parkhead. George McCluskey got the other Celtic goal to send the Parkhead fans home deliriously happy. That was the season when Celtic beat Rangers 4–2 in the last League game to go on and win the title, and Tom was immense.

Harry McCann, Coatbridge

MY best night of all in the Jungle didn't cost me a penny in admission and there wasn't a ball kicked! It was 26 May 1967, and the Lisbon Lions came home, proudly showing off the European Cup and giving those of us who couldn't get to Portugal an unforgettable night. There were over 60,000 of us there and the Jungle atmosphere was at least as good as anything ever seen there before. Carry-outs were still allowed in those days and the 'Champagne' kept me going until we had to leave Parkhead and head for a celebration dance in St Gerard's halls in Govan.

Tommy Flannigan, Penilee

JOCK STEIN showed his dry sense of humour right in line with the Jungle crowd at a celebrity match played before the Celtic–Manchester United testimonial for Bobby Lennox and Jimmy Johnstone. Billy Connolly, one of the showbiz stars in action, went down, either injured or just plain tired. As he was being stretchered off Stein, who must have had other things to think about, came running out of the tunnel and made the sign of the cross over the Big Yin.

Phil O'Brien

JOCK STEIN was never other than a big stopper centre-half for Celtic, which was strange when you consider the influence he was to have in later years as Celtic put the emphasis on fast, attacking play with entertainment high on the agenda. He rarely scored goals from his defensive role, but I remember his first when he grabbed a late equaliser against Hibs in season 1953–54. The big man had come from Welsh football late in 1951 and had made an immediate impact with his presence, dwarfing even men of the stature of great players such as Bobby Evans, Bertie Peacock, John McPhail and Charlie Tully. Big Jock showed them his managerial qualities even then by moulding those around him into a fine team and he became a big favourite with the Jungle fans with his trademark being his knee – which he used to make unorthodox clearances which landed at the halfway line.

It was no surprise when, within two years of his arrival, Celtic enjoyed their best season in very many years when they won the League and Cup double. As I say, the Big Man did not score too many goals but I was there when he got his first and it was a vital one, for it gave Celtic a 2–2 draw with Hibs at Parkhead that season. The Hibs team had all their big names, with Gordon Smith and Lawrie Reilly among them. Indeed, it was Reilly who got their two goals after Bobby Collins had put Celtic ahead. But Big Jock came to the rescue with his first goal for the club and that gave Celtic a precious point as they marched on to a title win – their first since 1938.

Harry O'Donnell

CHARACTERS are what football entertainment is all about and, luckily, at Parkhead we have always had a plentiful supply of them. For me, one of the best and certainly the biggest, was John 'Yogi' Hughes, who gave us a lot of fun and excitement from his first appearance as a 17-year-old in 1960 until he left for Crystal Palace in 1971. Yogi had some memorable days, but one I'll always remember was in January 1965 when he ran amok, scoring five against Aberdeen in an 8–0 win. The big man wore baseball boots that day as Parkhead was like an ice-rink but his balance would have been envied by Torvill and Dean.

Tom Brown, Coatbridge

BOBBY COLLINS might have been only 5 feet 4 inches tall, but he was a big man for Celtic and his great runs down the side of the Jungle made him a great favourite with the punters. After ten good years with us he left for Everton and then helped make Leeds United the great team they were to become. But it is his days scampering down the right wing that I'll always remember, and I thank the 'wee barra' for them.

Pat O'Brien, Govanhill

Talk About Embarrassment!

I TOOK my friend, a keen Celtic supporter but also a Church of Scotland minister, to see one of the games a few years ago. We were a few minutes late in arriving but soon made our way to the usual vantage spot where two other friends of mine were already in midstream, going on about the referee's parentage and organisation membership. During a brief break in their verbals to the match official, one friend asked if I was not going to introduce my companion. I replied that I hadn't been able to get in a word before but we soon exchanged names. After a further outburst at the man in the middle of the action, one of my pals stopped and said to the newcomer: 'And what do you do Tom?' to which my friend replied, 'Actually I'm a Church of Scotland Minister.' The abuse of the referee ended abruptly there as my first friend started a frantic search for a hole in the ground in which to bury his red face.

Jimmy Mac, Coatbridge

MY pal's teenage daughter was recovering from a severe bout of whooping cough a few years ago and we decided we would give her a treat to cheer her up.

'Anything I want?' she asked.

'Anything,' said we.

'Right,' she said, 'I want to go to Celtic Park and to the Jungle because that's the nearest you get to the team.'

Now, we are Jungle people anyway so that's where we would have taken her. But her mum intervened, saying she was in no fit state to be going anywhere, let alone standing on the terracing watching Celtic. But the girl's peruasive tongue and her wish to get near enough to see her hero, Derek Whyte, got her mum turned round. And in the end we were ordered to take her to the game.

That was okay until nearly half time when the packed Jungle was almost blown away by one of her loudest ever whoops. It seemed it was not quite out of her system yet. And that coughing fit must have registered high on the Richter Scale. You should have seen the Jungle scatter. You would have thought one of John Greig's clearances had landed there. But she was quite happy: she saw big Derek, Celtic won, and me and my pal earned some well-merited Brownie points from our wives.

John Sullivan

CELTIC fans are to be found in almost every corner of the globe and the one thing they have in common is they never forget their roots. Although they may be perfectly satisfied with life in new surroundings, the one thing they miss is going to Parkhead to see their favourites.

That is certainly the case for brothers James and Harry Owens, formerly of Baillieston, Glasgow, who are settled in a Sydney suburb with wives Maureen and Marie and their children. Harry writes: 'Both James and I are kept busy working here and we have a lovely lifestyle. The children are settled at school and doing well and I am enjoying myself playing football with Concord Amateurs. Everything would be terrific if we could only get to see Celtic. We have the next best thing with a local Celtic supporters club showing films of past glories and we see games on television or if families send tapes. But it's not the same as being in the Jungle where I used to stand. Our hopes were raised last season when Liam Brady was trying to arrange a tour of Australia for Celtic and we were shattered when it failed to materialise. Anyway, I have written a wee piece about the Jungle, so here goes:

'"Paradise Lost" – The Jungle to me was the heart of Celtic Park, a sacred place, an institution, a meeting place, a place of worship. As a young boy I learned to sing (chant) the hymns of our blessed Celtic and in doing so I became educated in more ways than one. When they put seats in the Jungle they called an end to an era. No more would we stand shoulder to shoulder as famous choir boys – like being in our cathedrals in Rome. But while we were in the Jungle, we lived our lives to the full. We have become a chapter in Celtic's history.'

Harry Owens, Sydney Celtic Supporters Club, Australia

CHAPTER NINE

Jungle Fans' Value – by the Bosses

DAVIE HAY perfectly summed up the effect the Jungle has on players by saying you never really appreciated it until you had left it behind. And his views are solidly backed by Billy McNeill, Lou Macari and Liam Brady. Billy, Lou and Davie speak from years of experience of being roared on and elevated to great heights by the Jungle's acclaim. And all three speak not only as former players but also from the managerial point of view.

Davie Hay says: 'I suppose, looking back on it, I was very fortunate to be playing with such quality players. We had skill, ability and flair all through the team, and when I played at right-back I counted myself the luckiest of all as I played right behind Jimmy Johnstone. Charging down that flank gave me a great chance to see the wee man at his best, in full flight. And it was a sheer delight to hear how the Jungle punters reacted to his amazing skills. Every time Jimmy got the ball you could feel the excitement rising from the Jungle. It started as a cheer and rose to a crescendo as they got behind the wee man. I was privileged to have a close-up not only of him but of his array of fans who just loved his every move.

'There is no doubt that the fans in there lifted you when you most needed their help. I've lost count of the times when they came to our rescue. It used to be said that the Celtic fans were worth a goal of a start and I've got to agree with that. When I came back there as manager I felt their presence was very important. To me the Celtic fans are, without a doubt, the finest vocal support in the world. It was only when I moved away to play with Chelsea and later to different management posts that I realised what I was missing. They were truly fantastic, and very special people, and I miss them very much. But I would like to place on record my thanks to them, first of all for their support during my playing career and secondly during my term as manager. They were an extra arm to me and I will forever remember them with great gratitude.'

Liam Brady travelled the world in a playing career in which he was ranked as one of the all-time greats. His midfield skills were lauded in England, first with Arsenal and latterly with West Ham. In between times he won over the highly critical Italian fans with his vision and finesse with giants such as Juventus, Inter Milan and Sampdoria. Always 'Celtic minded', Liam recalls the reception he received on visits there in the opposition ranks. The first was in August 1978 when the Gunners won 3–0. Next time round was much more meaningful, when a Juventus team packed with some of the top names in the business came to Parkhead on European Cup duty and attracted a crowd of 60,017. It was in September 1981 and Murdo MacLeod took the honours as the only scorer in the game. But Brady got his own back in the return when he masterminded Juventus to a 2–0 win before 70,000 in the Stadio Communale. Liam remembers: 'I'll never ever forget the reception I got from the Celtic fans in the first game with Juventus. It was quite staggering for a visiting player to be greeted in such a way. Those fans were truly exceptional and that occasion is filed away in my memory as one of the real highlights of my career. I always knew they were special people, however, as I had followed Celtic's fortunes as a wee boy in Dublin and throughout my playing career. I confess I still do follow the team's exploits and my only regret is that it did not work out for me in Glasgow. But the team will always have a special place in my affection.

'When I came to Glasgow as manager I was already familiar with the place, thanks to those earlier visits, and it was great to see the Jungle was still the place the fans loved to be. The fans there earned their place in Celtic's history and folklore and it is a pity that progress has had to be made at the expense of the removal of such a special area.'

Liam obviously has very special memories of life at Highbury from his glory days with Arsenal – and especially of his rapport with the occupants of the North Bank, which was the London equivalent of Celtic's Jungle. In Tom Watt's book *The End*, which covered 80 years of life on the North Bank terracing, you can sense his love of the old standing area now gone. He recalled: 'When you were playing at Highbury, that was what told you whether the ground was full or not. If you looked up at the North Bank and they were packed right up at the back, you knew there was no space in the whole ground. You knew you were playing in front of 60,000, which we'd get while I was playing there. We were a Cup team more than a League team. We never really got in a challenge for the League in the time I was there. We were always fourth or fifth. One season I think we were actually on top at Christmas but our challenge petered out. I think that on a week-to-week basis it's when your supporters believe you can win the League they really get behind you. We got to three consecutive Cup finals. The semi-finals are at a neutral ground and the final at Wembley so I can't ever remember celebrating anything great in front of the North Bank, which is a pity.'

He was denied this same opportunity at Parkhead, although he did enjoy some success – most notably the comeback to beat Cologne in the UEFA Cup in his first season. But he said: 'I only wish I had been given the chance to see the fans, especially the diehards in the Jungle at their very best. It must have been really special in the days of nine Championship wins in a row and in the run-up to winning the European Cup. That atmosphere and the rapport between team and supporters are what football is all about. That's what makes it the game it is. Still, I can't complain, I've enjoyed my time in the business and I'll always treasure the memory of that reception the Celtic fans gave me in my days with Juventus.'

The activities and memories of Billy McNeill are well documented elsewhere but no account of Celtic managers would be complete without the record-breaking captain's comments.

According to Billy: 'The Jungle was a unique place with an atmosphere all of its own. There is no question that its influence is missed. I know many of the fans have gone to other parts of the stadium but that very fact means they are being dispersed and that has diluted the effect they have on the games. When they were all packed together in the old Jungle area the impact they had on the games was incredible.'

Lou Macari also mourns the passing of the old place and feels the bulk of the passion has gone from football with the disappearance of the standing areas: 'I'll never forget the sight that greeted you when you ran out on to the park. It was just a mass of green and white and a sea of faces in the Jungle and the noise from there was incredible. I have no doubt that even the great teams of the past owed a lot to the Celtic fans in general and the Jungle in particular for roaring them home. Many of the European ties were close affairs and I am sure the Jungle fans played a major part in Celtic's great home record.'

Macari, who had a tremendous scoring record, netting eight goals in a dozen European ties, shared a love of the big games in the evening with the Parkhead fans. 'There was something really special about the glamour games in Europe and the atmosphere created by the fans was really inspirational.'

Lou went on to enjoy great success with Manchester United, playing before the famed Stretford End, but although he had a fine rapport with the Reds, it is his days as a player at Parkhead that he will remember with great fondness.

NEW manager Tommy Burns, who succeeded Lou Macari in July 1994, has his memories of the Jungle well documented elsewhere in this book. But super-enthusiast Tommy fully merits his place in this chapter as a former star who went on to become the ninth manager in Celtic's 106-year history. Tommy leans heavily on the support the fans give his men and makes no rash promises about a speedy return to trophy collecting.

He says: 'In my time as a Celtic player I never failed to admire how the fans gathered for every match to inject their passionate enthusiasm into the whole proceedings. All I ask is that they continue to provide the incredible volume of support to me in my new capacity as manager and to the team as we strive together to restore the good old days.'

From Norway to Paradise

WHEN I arrived in Glasgow from my native Norway in 1971 to study at university, I was already a Celtic supporter because of the great European Cup victory over Inter Milan in 1967. I arrived in Scotland on a Friday night and next morning travelled from Paisley by train to Glasgow. I arrived in the Central station and wanted to go to see

Celtic as soon as possible. I had learned English at High School in my own country and I thought my command of the English language was pretty good until I popped into a pub in Glasgow that Saturday morning. I could have been in Greece, or any other country you care to mention. Fortunately, some Glaswegians understood me, which is just as well as I didn't understand a word of Scottish.

Somehow I got down to Argyle Street and managed to get on a bus towards Parkhead. But as soon as I saw some of the Celtic brigade walking along the road I jumped off to follow them to be sure of getting to the ground. I had to walk for what seemed like ages, but that was a nice experience for me as I had never been to the United Kingdom before and I didn't know anything about the atmosphere regarding football matches in the UK. It was indeed a very new and very different experience for me. You seemed so dedicated and devoted to football, with the game on Saturday being the top event of the whole week. How could it be like that, I thought? I had never seen anything like this before, didn't realise how strongly people felt about the game. It took me some time to digest it, but I fully understand it now, many years later.

In any case, I ended up in the middle of the Jungle in my very first match in Glasgow. What a start for a foreigner not being able to understand anything of what people were saying, shouting and singing. For the first quarter of an hour I was so astonished and amazed at what was going on around me that I did not see very much of what happened on the park. I was more or less hypnotised by what was happening in the Jungle. What spirit, interest, knowledge, excitement, intensity, loyalty and overall support for Celtic. I found it unbelievable. These people, I thought, would fight to the death to support Celtic if they had to. It took me a while to really fully understand what was happening at that time but it was a kind of feeling I had to experience at first hand to get it into the blood where it still is and it is a very good feeling.

Before going to Scotland I was told (and taught) that Scottish people were miserly and not very friendly. But what I experienced that very first time in the Jungle, and since then of course, was quite the opposite. In the Jungle, supporters had plenty of carryouts and I was offered drink all the time. Obviously I got pissed, but who cares? I didn't at that time and people took care of me.

What really surprised me in the Jungle was the age of some of the supporters, some of them were more or less just infants. They couldn't speak or walk, but they got the right feeling into their veins from their fathers and the rest of the crowd. I suppose they picked up the body language pretty soon, anyway I did. The first time in the Jungle was instant swearing for me and I tell you the vocabulary was much bigger than I thought.

My impression of the Jungle was so big I couldn't really digest it but it was the right place for me. It is something that just has to be experienced, not simply spoken of. After that first match, at which Celtic beat Hibs 3–1, I went to the University Union bar with a lot of Celtic supporters and although I tried to buy a round of drinks for the people I was with, I never succeeded.

I am not a person to fawn over anyone, but after spending four years in Glasgow, before returning home, I must be honest and say there is no one to beat Glaswegians in respect of friendliness and generosity. You are simply the greatest and the best. My time in your city was well spent, with regards to my studies, too.

And one thing I will never forget is the sight of little Jinky Johnstone flying down the wing. When I returned home on visits, and then finally for good, I told all my friends of the great days at the Jungle and of J. Johnstone and others. He was my all-time favourite and I now have his own special video of all the great games and never tire of watching it. With some of my friends I have formed a Jimmy Johnstone appreciation society and had the honour of telling the members of the great times I spent at Parkhead. We showed the video and all had a terrific time. I still think fondly of my times in Glasgow and I am sad to hear that the Jungle is now merely a memory – but what a great memory, at least for me.

S. Olav Lie, Larvik, Norway

THERE was only one place I wanted to be for Davie Provan's testimonial match in November 1987 and that was in beside my pals in the Jungle. I was with the club at that time but I wanted to be in there with the lads, savouring the atmosphere. Unfortunately, there was a massive queue and by the time I got in Davie, who was still suffering from the ME illness which finished his career, had left the field. That was obviously a big disappointment but it was still great to be there with my mates, paying tribute to Davie.

The Jungle, up to that time, had always been my favourite viewing spot and from the age when I was allowed to go to games on my own I always stood in the Jungle. I'd jump on the train at Coatdyke station and get off at Carntyne and walk the rest of the way. I have many great memories of the Jungle as a supporter and one of them was the night the whole place was heaving when we beat Sporting Lisbon 5–0 after coming back from 2–0 down in the first leg.

As a player, my memories revolve round the Old Firm games but one goal I remember was against Hearts in a 3–0 win when I had come on as a substitute. I'll never forget running to the Jungle, and seeing those tightly packed fans acclaim my goal was an incredible feeling. Mind you, it was the sight of my teeth in photographs and television replays which set the lads off calling me Trigger – so it's not as if I have much chance of forgetting that goal.

Great days and great memories.

Gerry Creaney

TIGER TIM poured himself a glass of specially prepared Jungle Juice – green, of course – and mourned the end of the part of Parkhead he loved.

The radio DJ who once worked as an announcer for the club recalls: 'The box where I broadcast from stared right into the Jungle and the atmosphere that place generated was incredible. The fans in there set the mood for the rest of the ground and, for me, that was the place that made Parkhead really come alive. It was a sad moment when the fans had to make their last stand in there. You just couldn't beat the Jungle for the noise and sense of occasion and that's the place where the real characters emerged from at Celtic Park.

I remember once going round the park on a float. As I came to the Jungle, naturally enough, a lot of the fans started shouting jokey abuse at me so to get back at them I lifted my jumper to bare my chest. Instantly hundreds of fans yelled together, 'Tiger Tim's a baldy.' It could only have happened there.

It was a magical place and the fans in that area were incredible.'

I Sold Programmes in the Jungle on Danny's Big Night

WITH the Celtic Boys Club games being played on a Saturday, it was not very often I got to the weekend games, so when I did manage it was a very special feeling for me. When I was a wee boy my grandad always took me to the Rangers End but, with a bit of gentle persuasion, I got him to drift nearer the Jungle area as I always thought that was the place to be. When I was allowed to go with my pals it was always the Jungle we went to – although we never told anyone at the time.

But I remember one night being allowed to go there on official business – and it was a fantastic feeling. I was all dressed up in my Celtic Boys Club blazer and flannels – selling programmes. The occasion still sticks out in my mind as it was Danny McGrain's testimonial match against Manchester United in August 1980. It was brilliant.

As I say, because of playing for the Boys Club I only got in at the finish of games on Saturdays, so the games that stand out for me were those great European nights spent in the Jungle with my Coatbridge pals. They were magic.

I have been very lucky to have shared both experiences: being in there among the fans cheering on the team and then, later, being on the park – something I always consider a privilege, being cheered by the fans. I must say the Jungle has always been an inspiration to me and to many other Celtic players I have spoken to about it. And one of my best memories is not the day I made my début against Rangers as a substitute at Ibrox – although that was something very special – it was a week later when I ran out to face the Jungle for the first time as a first-team player right from the start to play against Hibs.

And another occasion that will live with me forever, and makes the hair stand up on the back of my neck when I think of it, was when it looked as though I might have to leave Celtic to find financial security for my family. Anyone who knows me will be well aware that having to leave Celtic would have been a heartbreak for me. And I think the fans know that I am one of them. If I had not been granted the privilege of playing for Celtic I would have been there in the

Jungle, roaring on the boys. Anyway, that day in particular was the last home game of the season and, although we had not won anything, the fans were giving us a rousing send-off and I was in the bath when a policeman came in and said the fans were chanting my name and were not going to leave until I went out to see them. Honest to God, I could not believe it. There were the fans, where I had stood, shouting for me. I have never felt so humble or so honoured and that is a feeling that will stay with me for the rest of my life.

Peter Grant

I SUPPOSE I am no different from countless other Celtic supporters who have special memories of the Jungle, but forgive me for thinking mine are that wee bit more special. For they are very personal and both are connected with my great hero, Jimmy Johnstone, who is to me the finest entertainer I have ever seen on a football field. Jimmy had always been my favourite player from when I was old enough to stand tip-toed on the Jungle steps to see him in action. I'll never ever forget that wee dip of the shoulder followed by one of his cheeky nutmegs, or a twisting and turning run from the wee man who was to me, and always will be, simply the best. When I was a youngster I didn't want to be like Jimmy Johnstone, I wanted to *be* Jimmy.

When his joint testimonial with Bobby Lennox was staged, I thought it was going to be my last ever chance of talking to the great man himself. That date is indelibly inscribed in my brain: 17 May 1976, with Manchester United supplying the opposition. It was a marvellous occasion but I was saddened to think the wee man, who had given me so much pleasure with his displays over the years, would be gracing the Jungle touchline for the last time.

At that time I was just turned 16 years old and was supposed to be an adult. I know it was wrong of me but, honestly, I just could not resist it. When Jimmy and Bobby were doing their lap of honour I had this irresistible urge to shake Jimmy's hand for what I thought would be the last time on that stage he had brought to life for us so often and so gloriously. With one leap I was over the top and with one bound I was by his side. The wee man was great and for me it was one of the finest moments of my life. There I was shaking hands with my hero and telling him what a fantastic game he had played and thanking him for all my great memories. It was fantastic. It was only when I turned and saw the sea of green and white in the Jungle that it sunk in what I had done. But that fleeting moment brought home to me what that vast sea of faces did for the players with their vocal encouragement.

Suddenly, I realised the eyes of the law were on me and I thought I was going to get lifted. Trying to be casual, I picked up my fallen scarf, dusted myself down and tried to stroll towards the Jungle. A cop was heading towards me and I thought, 'Oh, well, it was worth it just to shake hands with my idol.' But the young constable was brilliant. He gave me a pat on the back and escorted me back to the Jungle. Relief was instant for me, but it was possibly the worst thing the poor cop could have done, for within seconds other fans, seeing how leniently I had been dealt with, swarmed on to the track. It was soon sorted out, however, and years later I was still bumping into old mates from All Saints school who remembered me as the guy who was first on the park that night of Jimmy and Bobby's game.

My second memory brings me right up to date and I suppose could be called 'Jimmy, the sequel'. By then I was employed as a reporter with the *Celtic View* and when it was decided to mark the closure of the Jungle in style I staged a re-enactment of my handshake with Jimmy. Again, the wee man was magic. It was different because we were some 17 years older and the Jungle wasn't packed to capacity with fans all cheering him to the echo. But it was similar, too, for I was, and still am, in awe of that great wee player. He quickly put me at ease as we recalled that great night and the picture of me tackling him, this time in our suits, has pride of place in my household.

I'll never tire of telling people how Jimmy reminisced about his rapport with his 'favourite people' in the Jungle. Jimmy told me the testimonial night was one of the greatest nights of his life and he said standing on the Jungle steps with me just brought it back to him. As we spoke, I swear I could hear the roars of the fans as my mind went back to the great days and nights when Jimmy tore the opposition apart and I went home, tired and hoarse, but happy.

Joe Sullivan, *Celtic View*

POOR Frank Haffey has gone down in history for that unfortunate 'off-day' when he conceded nine goals to England but I, for one, would never change the big guy. He was a real happy-go-lucky character who gave us Celtic fans a lot of fun.

Some people conveniently forget about Frank's great displays both for Celtic and Scotland on other occasions. For instance, the year before the 9–3 defeat at Wembley, Frank had saved a blockbuster of a penalty from no less a player than Bobby Charlton and he did it again in a retake to prove it was no fluke. The game finished level at 1–1. I remember Frank volunteering to take a penalty against Airdrie and, okay, he missed it, but so what. Not many other keepers would have had the bottle to take it anyway. Another 'first' for Haffey was when he cut a record as a singer, and when he finished playing in Australia he entertained as a singer in a nightclub. Thanks, Frank, for some happy memories.

Tony Reilly, Coatbridge

There must have been a few dull matches watched from the Jungle over the years, I am sure. This was one of them. It was dull, deadly dull. Football was taking a back seat and the only thing sustaining us was the patter. From the back of the Jungle came a shout, 'Bring back Patsy Gallagher', to which there came the speedy riposte, 'Bring back Bridie Gallagher.'

John O'Brien

AFTER years of supporting the Bhoys from the Jungle, I moved south and went to a few of the bigger London games but, while I enjoyed the football, I missed the very special atmosphere I had grown up with. After a while I moved on to Liverpool and this took me a lot nearer home, and during one of my trips to Glasgow I was taken on a conducted tour of Celtic Park. The most memorable part of this was when we walked out of the players' tunnel and my eye automatically turned to my own part of the Jungle. A few memories came back that day and I admit a few tears were shed as well.

Gary Scott, Liverpool

THE first game I played for Celtic was against Hibs at Parkhead and Billy McNeill, who was the manager, had held me back as the teams ran out, and then sent me out on my own. I felt like a prat, but it was a great feeling getting that special cheer to myself. But it was also a bit strange because I used to stand in the Jungle and watch them.

Frank McAvennie, *Once a Tim*

BRIAN was 17 years old at the time and as committed to the Celtic cause as any good Bridgeton teenager should be. As usual he left the house near Bridgeton Cross at two o'clock this winter afternoon to go to the game against Hibs at Parkhead. When he did not come straight home for his tea we were not too concerned – at first. Then we began to worry. His dad and I started to look for him about the neighbourhood that night and, while we were out, I bought an early edition of the Sunday paper just in case there had been an accident at the game or something else had happened. We were still not too worried as, although he was only 17 years old, Brian was capable of looking after himself. On the front page of the paper was a 'fun-story' showing a picture of a big policeman on the track at Tynecastle where Rangers had been playing Hearts. The cop had his hat in his hand, dusting some snow off it, and the story told of the fun and frolics as the fans threw snowballs about. One had obviously struck bullseye but the policeman had taken it in good fun.

But then we went home, and much later I answered the door to find two policemen looking for Brian's mother. I told them I was she and was shattered to hear them say, 'Brian's in a cell at Tobago Street police station, missus. He's being charged with breach of the peace for throwing a snowball at a policeman.' And to think I always defended our policemen – saying Glasgow police were the best in the country! Poor Brian must have got the one exception to the rule, whereas a similar incident in Edinburgh would have been treated entirely differently.

For obvious reasons I must remain nameless

CHAPTER TEN

Tully's Tricks Went Down a Treat – Neil Mochan

ACCORDING to Neil Mochan, the Jungle fans quite literally had 'tunnel vision' in his great days as a player at Parkhead. And their support was invaluable even to a team that boasted such stars as Charlie Tully, Bobby Evans, Willie Fernie and John McPhail. In an interview just weeks before his death in August 1944, Neil explained: 'In those days we used to run out the old tunnel which covered the entrance to the playing pitch. We were hidden from the view of everyone, except those right opposite us in the Jungle, until we hit the track. But the Jungle fans could see right up the tunnel from across the park and knew exactly when we were coming out and their ear-splitting roar let everyone else know and the shout echoed round the entire stadium. We were always guaranteed a warm welcome from the fans, no matter where they were standing, but I have to say the guys in the Jungle were a bit special. They knew their football, too, and gave us terrific backing. Even if you were having an off-day they were behind you, just as long as they knew you were giving it every-thing you had. They had no time for any shirkers though and soon let anyone know, no matter who they were.

'But, like everything else in football, they had their favourites and Charlie Tully could do no wrong as far as they were concerned. Charlie was some stuff, right enough, and his tricks went down a real treat with the Jungle fans. Some of the tricks he used to get up to were marvellous to watch but, as well as being clever on the ball, he was also a great player who could open up defences with one move. And every time the ball came to Charlie there was a buzz about the place as no one knew what he was going to do but they knew he would try something different every time.

'I suppose I was fortunate, too, for playing so near them on the wing, and sometimes at left back, meant I was right there for the Jungle to see and because I had such a hard shot I was soon established as a favourite with them.

'Mind you, I had heard all about the fans before I played in front of them as a Celtic player. When I signed from Middlesbrough in May 1953 my first few games were at Hampden before I had even played at Parkhead. The team had qualified for the Glasgow Charity Cup final by beating Clyde and Third Lanark just before I arrived and, in my first game for Celtic, we beat Queen's Park 3–1 in the final. I scored twice and Willie Fernie got our other goal that day. We then went on to play in the Coronation Cup and, after beating Arsenal 1–0, with a Bobby Collins goal, we beat Manchester United 2–1 and I scored one of our goals with Bertie Peacock getting the other. The final was fantastic, for I scored the first, which I'm happy to say is talked about yet, and Jimmy Walsh got the other one in a 2–0 victory. So that was me a Celtic player with two Cup winners medals won inside three weeks and I had not even kicked a ball at Parkhead yet.'

Even more incredibly, Mochan had been seen by 281,600 fans in those four games as the attendance for the Charity Cup clash with Queen's Park had been 20,600. Then on the Monday night, 60,000 turned up expecting to see English champions Arsenal score an easy victory. They were wrong and so, too, were Manchester United who went into the semi-final with Celtic on the back of a 2–1 win over Rangers in their first tie. A crowd of 73,000 watched as Celtic beat a star-studded United side packed with household names such as Crompton, Carey, Rowley and Pearson. But they were swept aside as Celtic set up a final with Hibs and the Famous Five of Smith, Johnston, Reilly, Turnbull and Ormond.

That Mochan 'special' is indelibly inscribed in the minds of those in the 108,000 crowd privileged to have witnessed it and the distance gets further away from goal the more the story is told. It was a well-directed clearance from Jock Stein that started the move and when Willie Fernie turned it into Mochan's path the centre-forward simply hammered it past Tommy Younger to give the big keeper not an earthly. Charlie Tully perhaps summed up

Mochan best by saying: 'Neilly had a cannonball shot. When Fernie, Collins and myself were stroking the ball about to each other, jockeying for position, Neilly would bawl across to us, "Never mind the patting and messing about with the ball. Get it over here and I'll do the rest." There's just no arguing with that.' Neilly's wait to appear before the Jungle proved well worth while for, although he played only 22 league games that first season, he managed 20 goals as Celtic strode to their first League title since 1937–38. He also scored four goals on the way to the Scottish Cup win over Aberdeen.

Neil says: 'There is no doubt those were great times and, on many occasions, we had to rely on the fans to lift us and inspire us to victory. Make no mistake about it, those Jungle fans made some difference both in my days and, later, to even greater times like the Lisbon Lions, a side that was packed full of characters the Jungle fans loved. When games were tough they had the ability to inspire with their unbelievable support and, when you were on top, they were just as enthusiastic so you were on a winner either way. It was an each-way bet that was a sure winner.'

Nearing the end of his playing career with Celtic, Neil was switched to left-back, where he played with distinction, but on one occasion he reverted to centre-forward in a Scottish Cup tie against St Mirren and scored all five goals in a 5–0 win at Parkhead. Incredibly, this was a replay after the teams had tied 4–4 five days earlier, when Neil and John Divers got two goals apiece. Modestly, Neilly says: 'Aye, I got five that day. It wisnae a bad effort.' His playing career at Parkhead ended in November 1960 when he moved to Dundee United and he finished playing with Raith Rovers in season 1963–64. However, he was not lost to Celtic, for he returned as assistant trainer/coach in 1964 and stayed there until his death.

And one of the most talked about goals, which each new set of arrivals on the playing staff never tire of hearing about, is that great 30-, or was it 35-, or maybe even 40-yarder in that great Coronation Cup final on 20 May 1953.

One Shout From the Jungle Won Us the League

THE fans who occupied the Jungle deservedly won praise over the years for their non-stop support and incredible vocal backing, but one player in particular is convinced they played a major part in winning at least one League Championship. He is Bobby Lennox, the buzz-bomb winger who participated in every one of Celtic's stunning nine-in-a-row championship run.

Said Bobby: 'It came in the second-last League game in season 1967–68 when ourselves and Rangers were running neck and neck for the title. They had beaten us 1–0 in the second League game of the season when Orjan Persson scored the only goal of the game at Ibrox. We went all the way without losing another but Rangers were doing even better as they were still unbeaten going into the late stages. Then came the turning point, when they dropped a point in a no-scoring draw with Dundee United at Tannadice. And that gave us the chance of a breakthrough.

'It happened in a midweek game when we were playing Clyde in the Glasgow Cup final at Hampden while Rangers were on League business at Cappielow. We were winning 7–0 at half time with myself scoring three, John Hughes two and Jimmy Johnstone and Tommy Gemmell getting the others. But the drama came at half time when big Jock Stein came into the dressing-room to say Rangers were 2–0 down to Morton at half time in their game. It was truly unbelievable and we wondered if it was true, as sometimes the big man would wind us up by giving us the score the wrong way round. This time it was true and even when Bobby Murdoch completed our scoring to make it 8–0 our minds were on what was happening at Cappielow. We heard first of all it was 3–2 and then it had finished at 3–3. We were beside ourselves with joy as we had won the Glasgow Cup and were now on top of the League on goal difference. What a night!

'But there was still more work to be done as we had to face Morton at Parkhead on the Saturday while Rangers made the trip to Rugby Park to meet Kilmarnock. It was still anybody's title but we were determined to hold on to the Championship no matter what happened. That second dropped point by Rangers had given us a slight advantage and we were out to make the most of it. Willie Wallace gave us an early goal against Morton and the crowd of 51,000 went wild with delight. But Morton showed that their fight-back against Rangers had been no fluke and Joe Mason got an equaliser. It stayed that way into injury time and it was in those dying seconds that a fan in the Jungle won the title for us. As I ran towards the Jungle to take a throw-in, a fan shouted out to me, "Bobby, Rangers are winning 2–1 at Kilmarnock – they're going to win the League." I laid the ball down and raced into the middle to get ready for the throw-in and when it came Willie Wallace missed it and I made contact. It was not the best goal I have ever scored but it was one of the most vital. The ball went under the keeper's body as he dived and seconds later the referee blew for time up. We all went mad. And to this day I say that if that fan had not told me the scoreline from Kilmarnock I would probably not have raced into the middle to get that chance. His shout put us once more in the driving-seat, for Rangers had indeed won 2–1 and we were still ahead on goal average.

'Again, though, it was not all over, for Rangers had to play Aberdeen at Ibrox while we went to Dunfermline. Our game was postponed that Saturday as the Fifers were in the Scottish Cup final against Hearts, having put us out in the first round. Big Jock took us to Seamill to prepare for the game with Dunfermline at East End Park on the following Tuesday but he let us go to Hampden for the final. Dunfermline won 3–1 but we left early to get back to Seamill and heard on the radio that Rangers had lost to Aberdeen. It was 3–2 at home and it was their one and only League defeat of the season.

'Now the stage was set for the showdown and we knew it would have taken a landslide victory by the Fifers to rob us of the title. But there was a lot at stake, for we wanted to do it in style and, at the same time, take revenge on the new Cup holders for putting us out so early in the competition. Pat Gardner scored first for them amid pandemonium. Thankfully, I got the equaliser just after the interval and went on to get the winner to retain the title.

'But I will never ever forget the part played by that punter who gave us the spur to get the one that made all the difference against Morton in that second-last match.'

Modesty, of course, forbids Bobby from taking his share of the credit for the title win although the shout from the Jungle was obvi-ously of great significance. But in the run-in to the title Bobby scored in every one of the final dozen games, a staggering 20 goals in all in the run, including a hat-trick against Aberdeen and four against St Johnstone. That took his league total to 32 goals in 28 appearances and to that you can add seven in nine League Cup games and three in the Glasgow Cup final, a grand total of 42 goals. Mark you, scoring goals was a way of life for the wee man born in Saltcoats in 1943. In 537 domestic League and Cup games for Celtic he scored no fewer than 272 goals.

But, inevitably, it was one that got away that annoyed him more than any other. It happened in the second leg of the European Cup Winners Cup semi-final against Liverpool at Anfield in April 1966. Lennox had scored the only goal of the game to give them a slender lead to take to Merseyside and after Tommy Smith and Geoff Strong had given Liverpool the lead on aggregate, Lennox scored the goal which should have put Celtic into the final on the away-goals rule. It was chalked off and, at the finish, Bobby said one of the Liverpool players, although delighted to be in the final, put his arm around him and said Celtic had been robbed.

Much later, writing in his autobiography, *A Million Miles for Celtic*, Bobby said: 'A couple of weeks later, back on the safety of his own soil, the French referee had the nerve to admit in a magazine interview that he had made a mistake. There's no doubt in my mind his decision that night cost Celtic more than £100,000 because the final was due to be played at Hampden Park where Liverpool eventually lost to West German opposition.'

But if that was a bitter disappointment and undoubtedly one of the saddest nights of Bobby's long and distinguished career, one of the most poignant was in May 1976 when he and Jimmy Johnstone ran out together for the last time as Celtic team-mates. It was their joint testimonial against Manchester United and, although many fans felt they deserved a night each to themselves, it was decided they were so inseparable it was only right and proper for them to share the big occasion. Jimmy Johnstone speaks elsewhere of his golden memories of that great night and for Bobby, too, it was a night of great joy but also tinged with more than a fair bit of sadness.

Typically, it had rained all day and the two pals thought they would be lucky to get 10,000. They underestimated the feelings the vast Celtic support had for them as shown by the fact that 50,000 were there to give them a suitable send-off – well, for Jimmy, at least, as he had already left Celtic to join Sheffield United.

Bobby says: 'Kenny Dalglish had a great night, scoring three, and I got the other in a 4–0 victory, but it was the finish that meant so much to me. I'll never forget the sea of faces as wee Jimmy and I ran past the Jungle on our way round the track. Fans were throwing scarves at us and thousands more waved in an incredible scene of emotion. I was shattered, drained with it all and when we got back to the stand big Jock was there to tell us to go back round or the fans would never go away. This time we crossed the centre and Jimmy made a bee-line for the Jungle, a place where he was a huge favourite and the part of the ground he loved and played up to. As he ran wee Jimmy took off his boots and threw them into the Jungle to incredible applause.'

Like most fans, and he was a fan as much as a player, Bobby took great delight in the stunning 4–2 win over Rangers to clinch the League title in 1979 – but for an extra special reason. Bobby is in no doubt it was the greatest night at Parkhead since the return from Lisbon with the Cup and he cites good reason for this, saying it was the first time, including the great Jock Stein era, that the title had been clinched at Parkhead. 'For me that made it all the more special, for the players, the fans, and everyone associated with the club,' said Bobby. What also gave it an extra dimension for Bobby is that it came after Billy McNeill had brought him back into the scheme of things at Parkhead after he had left for a brief spell in American football. The previous year Bobby had shown he still had his shooting boots on by scoring 15 goals in 36 games for Houston Hurricanes, but that League winner's medal in 1979 to add to the nine-in-a-row and another in 1977 made his return all the more worth while.

Susan's Soccer Lessons

THE questions were seemingly endless as my girlfriend, Susan, and I made our way to Celtic Park that March night in 1967. Will the game go on? That was her main concern as I wondered why I had not succeeded in talking her out of coming to the game in the first place. All the old excuses had failed, such as not being able to get a seat in the stand and having to crush into the Jungle along with thousands of others. But Susan was a real trooper. Regardless of anything else, she wanted to be there on the big night and even the thought of a 75,000 crowd did not deter her. I made sure that she was well clued up that Vojvodina came from Yugoslavia and that we needed two clear goals to go through – and that Celtic were the team in the green- and-white hoops.

As we reached my usual spot in the Jungle I quickly realised that, although it was fine for me, Susan was at a distinct disadvantage with regards to her height. Let's get down to the front, was her response. Now, pushing your way through a big crowd has certain drawbacks. And as Susan was happily and excitedly weaving her way through the fans she soon found one of them. We got separated by a few yards. And as Susan spied what she thought was a good vantage point she turned and grabbed what she thought was my hand to guide me to her side.

It was not me. It was a complete stranger she had got hold of and was dragging through the packed Jungle. Luckily the middle-aged fan took it well, saying, 'And here I was thinking I was past it' to Susan just as I was emerging through the crowd. Susan was totally embarrassed but the man was delighted, telling her at least she had found him a good place.

The constant rain all night had made the place awash and the water was up to the height of the first step and everyone was keeping that wee bit back from it. But as the teams came out to a terrific welcome, we found ourselves being edged nearer the water mark. Susan's presence, however, had at least a good effect on the men around us as they suitably moderated their language and everything became flippin' this and flippin' that.

Jinky Johnstone was magic that night and Susan's comments brought wry smiles to the Jungle Jims as she told me, 'That's not fair, he's a cheat, he deliberately kicked that wee man with the red hair.' With about an hour gone, Stevie Chalmers scored to level the aggregate and Susan was in a state of near shock as I hugged her and she saw other grown men dancing about like wee boys with their arms around each other.

After much pressure, it was still stalemate, and all around us guys were saying it was heading for flippin' extra flippin' time. But, suddenly, Celtic had a corner and Charlie Gallagher seemed to take an hour to put the ball on the spot before sending over an inch-perfect cross for Billy McNeill to do the rest and head powerfully into the net. I swear the roar must have been heard in Cambuslang as bedlam broke out in the Jungle. The people at the front, ourselves and the rest of the flippin' fans, who had been avoiding the water at the bottom step, were now dancing in it like children at the seashore. The celebrating continued unabated when the final whistle sounded and a bedraggled and shaken Susan was screaming, 'Is that it? Have Celtic won the Cup now?'

I told her, 'No, not yet, but I've a feeling we might just flippin' well do it now.'

Michael McGinlay, Milton

NOSTALGIA hung heavily in the air on the afternoon of 12 March 1994, when Liverpool played hosts to near neighbours Everton for the last time in front of the Spion Kop. Like the Jungle, it was to fall victim to the calls for ground improvement and all-seater stadia through-out the country and Kopites, like the Jungle counterparts before them, had gathered to mourn its passing on derby day. More than 16,000 fans packed into the old area in Walton Breck Road, Liverpool, which has housed Liverpool fans since 1906. The red army tried hard to make it a really special occasion as they attempted to lift the roof with their vocal chords strained to the limit in umpteen verses of 'You'll Never Walk Alone'.

Marcello Mega, paying tribute in print the following Monday, wrote: 'The rendition of that song just after the sides emerged touched a few heartstrings. Jackie Downie, standing next to me, said, "Listen to that. You can't make that much noise sat on your arse!"' That said it all for the standing-room-only patrons. Marcello contin-ued: 'Earlier the Albert Bar, where many of the songs that helped build the Kop's fame had been penned over the years, was in unusu-ally sombre mood. Charlie Lee, a Kopite for 30 years, said, "It's not the end for the Kop yet, but it's games like this that bring it home. It's the last time we get to cheer the lads while they stuff the Blues. It's hard to believe."'

The great Bill Shankly had described the Kop's ability to 'suck the ball' into the net when Liverpool were on the attack and Craig Johnston said, after leaving the club in 1988, 'The Kop in its glory was an awesome thing, rising and roaring like a volcano obliterat-ing rival supporters and teams alike.'

When opened in 1906 it was named after the Spion Kop in South Africa where so many young Liverpudlians were killed in battle in the Boer War. The Liverpool fans, like their counterparts at Parkhead, took to the old area and attached themselves like leeches to the mountain of steps which seemed to rise into the sky.

In his homage after the final derby before compulsory seating,

Marcello wrote: 'In 1928, it was covered during a spell of prosperity for the club, and turned into the most intimidating cathedral of sound in England. Once holding as many fans as the rest of the ground combined, its appeal was enormous for generations of young supporters. The tragedies of Heysel and Hillsborough took their toll on the entire Merseyside community, but especially on Liverpool supporters. When the bell tolled for 95 Liverpool fans in Sheffield it signalled the end for the Kop. When numb supporters arrived at Anfield in the days after that tragedy and the gates were thrown open, the first group to enter headed for the Kop. It was the natural place for a shrine.'

The reaction to those tragedies resulted in the closure of the Jungle, the Kop, the Stretford Road End and the North Bank at Arsenal in particular and supporters of all four clubs are as one as they declare the atmosphere generated in those famous arenas will never be the same again.

Wingers were always very much an integral part of Celtic teams from as far back as I can remember and I have been going to the Jungle for almost 40 years. Bobby Collins, known as 'the wee barra' was the man for me in the late Fifties and he and Charlie Tully provided a great contrast in style and individuality. We have been lucky in the guys who used to parade their skills along the touchline on both the Jungle and stand sides. There was Jimmy Johnstone who was, for me, the greatest entertainer of them all. Since Davie Provan was unluckily forced to retire through illness we have suffered a dearth of good wingers. I will never forget Davie's magnificently struck free kick which gave us a kiss of life in the Scottish Cup final against Dundee United in 1985. Frank McGarvey caught Davie's lifeline and we went on to win with Frank's great diving header, after looking down and out before Provan struck. While I was sad at the premature end to his career I was pleased to see and hear that Davie's speed on the wing is matched by his quick wits on radio and television. He gave us a lot of fun in his playing days down that right wing and now provides us with expert analysis on the radio. Long may he continue as he is one 'expert' who really knows his subject.

Harry O'Donnell, Maryhill

THE first time I saw Roy Aitken I knew immediately this big lad was destined to be a great Celt and happily it turned out that way. Mind you, I should have known he would make it as, three years earlier when Roy was just 13 years old, Jock Stein had tipped him for the top saying, 'That boy will play for Scotland.'

As usual, Big Jock was proved right. And it was he who gave Roy his début in 1975 when he played in a League Cup tie against Stenhousemuir. But he had to wait until the following February, when he took the No. 5 jersey against Aberdeen, and retained it until the end of the season. Although he was just 16 he was already showing signs he was a player around whom a defence could be moulded. I watched him right from that start and was not surprised that he went on to make more than 600 appearances for Celtic before leaving for Newcastle in January 1990.

He was well named 'The Bear' by his fans in the Jungle, for Roy growled his way through a match, trying to inspire everyone around him by his own industry.

He had many fine games but I think his proudest achievement was in leading Celtic to the Centenary League and Cup double in 1988.

George McGhee

IN the second leg of the Partizan Belgrade match, Dariusz Dziekanowski became the first Celt ever to score four goals in one European match, and he still ended up on the losing side! Only four other Celtic players have scored hat-tricks in Euro ties. They are John Hughes, against Basle, Switzerland, in a 5–1 win in September 1963; Harry Hood, against Kokkola, Finland, 9–0 in September 1970; Willie Wallace, against Waterford, Republic of Ireland, 7–0 in October 1970; and Frank McGarvey, against DVTK, of Hungary, 6–0 in August 1980.

Celtic Programme, September 1991

IN any redevelopment of Celtic Park, the Jungle is the last place which we would want redeveloped, and if the staff cares about atmosphere being created, they would leave the Jungle well alone. Speaking of the board, we ask all of you: who will remain in the Jungle, to generate as much noise and atmosphere as possible and continue to chant and sing the songs that will encourage our team to victory? Nothing beats the Jungle in full flight, in full voice and in full colour. You know it makes sense.

Once a Tim, issue 16

MAKE no mistake about it, the fans in the Jungle are the finest judge of a player at Celtic Park. They know their football inside out and they recognise quality when they see it and give praise accordingly. We were lucky in my time there both as a player, first of all with such stars as Charlie Tully, and later as assistant manager to big Jock Stein, when we had the great Lisbon Lions team. Tully was a real character and the fans loved his every move. They really appreciated his style, ability and antics and Charlie played up to them at every turn. But the guys in there could make or break a player. If they took to you that was you made for life with them. If, on the other hand, they took a dislike to a player he faced a struggle for the rest of his career. You did not have to have great ability to make it with the Jungle fans, just as long as they knew you were giving 100 per cent at all times. If you shirked a tackle just once, though, you were done for with them. The white feather was a sign they had no time for.

I must say I was very fortunate with the fans in there, for they knew that I gave my all in every game and played to the best of the ability God had given me. I laugh now when I think they christened me 'The Iron Man' for I was only flesh and blood just like them and I think I broke just about every bone in my body in the cause. So much for the Iron Man. But I loved my time with Celtic and the fans were, and still are, to me the greatest in the world.

Sean Fallon

CHAPTER ELEVEN

Down Memory Lane – Ten Thrillers in the Jungle

THERE is nothing football fans like more than a good old-fashioned argument about the respective merits of players or an incident at a particular match. Everyone, it seems, has their favourite memory and certainly nostalgia rules when it comes to recalling them in print. My late, but very dear friend and former colleague Hugh Taylor, one of the old school of sports journalists, enjoyed nothing better than what he described as a wander down Memory Lane.

It was a similar venture which sparked off the germ of an idea for this book. On reading, in the *Celtic View*, that the Jungle was about to be consigned to the history books and memory banks, and declared a thing of the past, with seating taking over from the space where many thousands of Celtic fans had been weaned, I wrote an article in the *Evening Times* selecting what I considered to be my ten best games in the modern era. The reaction was astonishing; with many people agreeing, many disagreeing and everyone wanting to make their own point of view known.

For the record, here are the games as chosen by me. You may not agree with them all, but I am sure you will enjoy chewing over old memories. Certainly, the players who took part in them did, and some of them give their own recollections elsewhere in these pages.

17 May 1976

Two fans in particular had their days made for them at this match when Jimmy Johnstone made a bee-line for the Jungle and threw his boots into the crowd. Earlier, the lucky fans had joined in tumultuous applause as Celtic took a well-deserved bow after beating Tommy Docherty's Manchester United 4–0.

This was Jimmy Johnstone and Bobby Lennox's joint testimonial and, at the end of it, wee Bobby stayed back and sent his pal out to take his final salute from his massed ranks of admirers. Almost 50,000 had turned up to pay tribute to two of the best entertainers to ever wear the colours. And at 80 pence a head in the terracing they sure got their money's worth.

Bobby Lennox set the tone for a great night with a glorious header when even an ordinary header from the Buzz Bomb would be unique. But the man who captured the fans' attention was Davie Hay, with his powerful running and midfield domination. This was Davie's first game back at Parkhead since his £225,000 transfer to Chelsea in July 1974. Hay was tremendous and Kenny Dalglish ranked alongside, scoring a replica of his famous 'nutmeg' goal against Ray Clemence in Scotland's 2–1 win over England at Hampden. This time Alex Stepney was Kenny's victim and he followed this up, after combining with Jimmy Johnstone, by sending the cheekiest of lobs over Stepney. Dalglish then finished it off in style after excellent interplay with Johnny Doyle.

The teams – and these are sure to be the subject of much discussion – were:

> CELTIC: Latchford, McGrain, Lynch, Glavin, Edvaldsson, Hay, Johnstone, Doyle, Dalglish, Callaghan and Lennox.
> Substitutes: P. McCluskey, McDonald, Wilson and Burns.
> MANCHESTER UNITED: Stepney, Forsyth, Houston, Jackson, Waldren, Buchan, Coppell, McIlroy, McCreery, Loughnane, Storey.
> Substitutes: Albiston, Roche, Coyne and Paterson.

8 September 1973

Jock Stein was a pastmaster at exploiting even the most mundane events and, with his eye for the main chance, turning them to his advantage. This was clearly illustrated when he sent out his team to face Clyde in their first home match of the season in 1973 – 74.

Having just made it eight-in-a-row months earlier, Stein

decided something special was called for to generate interest before his team went flat out to make it a world-equalling nine successive titles.

Cleverly, and in a unique way emphasising their dominance of the Scottish scene, Big Jock warned the fans that something special would be happening. He kitted his entire team out in shorts bearing the number 8 in recognition of their achievement.

It took a trick with the fans and the team ran riot. Bobby Lennox grabbed a hat-trick to go along with goals by Kenny Dalglish and a rare one from his great pal Danny McGrain.

The teams were:

CELTIC: Hunter, McGrain, Brogan, Murray, McNeill, Connelly, McLaughlin (Johnstone), Hood (Wilson), Dalglish, Hay and Lennox.

CLYDE: Cairney, McHugh, Swan, Beattie, McVie, Ahern, Sullivan, Burns, Gillespie, McGrain and Miller.

2 November 1983

Frank McGarvey can always be relied on to come up with a colourful description of events associated with Celtic and he did not let me down when recalling the night Celtic demolished Sporting Lisbon.

Said Frank: 'We had lost 2–0 in the first leg and we got no more than we deserved as we were awful. They must have arrived in Glasgow thinking they were on their holidays. But it was a side vastly different in attitude they were facing this time. We were bursting to get at them and manager Davie Hay had literally to bar the door with his body as we were straining to get at them. It was the proverbial raw-meat stuff, but it added another dimension to the sheer quality of the play.'

Celtic had to wait until the 17th minute to make the breakthrough when Tommy Burns scored, but after that it was to be a case of 'how many' although the Portuguese were still offering stiff resistance at this stage. Then came two magnificent minutes which changed the entire course of events. Tom McAdam levelled on aggregate and right on half time Brian McClair put Celtic ahead for the first time in the tie. In the space of another two minutes, the 57th and 59th, Murdo MacLeod and Frank McGarvey settled it in some style for one of Celtic's finest ever victories.

The Celtic team was: Bonner, McGrain, Sinclair, Aitken,

McAdam, MacLeod, Provan, McStay, McGarvey (Melrose), Burns (Reid) and McClair.

8 March 1967

In a competition to find the most dramatic winner of all time at Parkhead, the one by Billy McNeill against Vojvodina Novi Sad must be a front runner and perhaps even odds-on favourite.

There were barely 20 seconds left on the clock when Caesar gave the Yugoslavs the thumbs down. The dramatic quarter-final tie in the European Cup appeared to be heading for a play-off in Rotterdam when big Billy struck. Steve Chalmers had equalised the goal the visitors had scored in the opening tie but time was quickly running out when the dramatic winner came out of the blue.

Jimmy Johnstone, who had tortured the visitors with some of his amazing skills, won a corner on the right and his captain ran upfield for the last-gasp, death-or-glory finish. Charlie Gallagher swung over the perfect corner and McNeill leapt high to head powerfully past keeper Pantelic. Parkhead simply exploded in an astonishing display of delight at qualifying for the semi-final stage.

Celtic's team was: Simpson, Craig, Gemmell, Murdoch, McNeill, Clark, Johnstone, Lennox, Chalmers, Gallagher and Hughes.

7 November 1984

Mention the name of Rapid Vienna to a Celtic supporter – and duck. Or at least be prepared for a vitriolic assault on your ears as the fan gets rid of some venom stored away as a result of this match.

Going into this one on the back of a 3–1 defeat in Austria there was obviously going to be some drama in store, but no one could have predicted the fiery outcome.

Brian McClair reduced the leeway to one goal when he netted in the 32nd minute and excitement was building by the second. Celtic were now going flat out for equality and eventual victory and, right on the half-time break, Murdo MacLeod sent one of his special rocket-boosted deliveries into the corner of the net to make it 3–3.

Frank McGarvey broke free to send Tommy Burns in on the keeper and when it bounced off the goalie's body Tommy turned it past him into the net. The Austrians protested bitterly and Burns was floored by Keinast outside the referee's vision. But the deed had been seen by the linesman and the Austrian was red-carded.

Peter Grant then sent a penalty just wide and, as the drama continued at fever pitch, Weinhofer went down as though struck by some ghostly hand. The Austrians indicated their man had been struck by a missile thrown from the Jungle but there was no evidence of this on television. And, after an appeal which was upheld by UEFA, the game was ordered to be replayed 200 miles from Parkhead and Celtic were beaten 1–0 to go out of the tournament.

The Celtic team was: Bonner, W. McStay, MacLeod, Aitken, McAdam, Grant, Provan, P. McStay, McClair, Burns and McGarvey.

21 May 1979

There was enough drama in the Old Firm game that day alone for a dozen games between the old rivals. Needing two points to snatch the title from Rangers' grip, Celtic were a goal behind after only nine minutes and a man short after 55.

Alex MacDonald swept Rangers into the lead and, despite great pressure from Celtic, that was how it remained until the 66th minute when Roy Aitken, who had been in inspirational form, equalised. Johnny Doyle had been given his marching orders earlier after an incident with MacDonald and Celtic sent on Bobby Lennox for Mike Conroy while Rangers replaced Tommy McLean with Alex Miller as fresh legs were required to cope with the onslaught.

Despite being a man down, Celtic continued to attack Rangers and George McCluskey got his reward with a goal in the 74th minute. But while Celtic fans were still celebrating Rangers hit back. Bobby Russell was the Rangers hero as he brought them level again, but with five minutes left Colin Jackson put through his own goal to give Celtic the lead once more and then Murdo MacLeod unleashed an unstoppable shot past Peter McCloy to make it 4–2.

This gave Celtic the title by 48 points to Rangers 45.

The teams were:

CELTIC: Latchford, McGrain, Lynch, Aitken, McAdam, Edvaldsson, Provan, Conroy, McCluskey, MacLeod and Doyle.

RANGERS: McCloy, Jardine, Dawson, Johnstone, Jackson, MacDonald, McLean, Russell, Parlane, Smith and Cooper.

27 September 1989

Mention the name of Partizan Belgrade and you automatically think of Dariusz (Jacki) Dziekanowski. Their names go hand in hand into the record books along with one of the most bitter-sweet nights in Celtic's recent history. For the neutrals there that night it must have been one of the most remarkable games ever witnessed at the stadium. For the Parkhead fans it was sheer full-blooded excitement mixed with shattering disappointment.

The memory of Jacki's drawn face with his unbelieving eyes will stay with me forever as the Polish international star summed up his feelings in two words: 'I sick!' And well he might have been, too, for Jacki ran amok that night against Ivan Golac's men, scoring four goals in the European Cup Winners Cup tie which Celtic won 5–4, only to go out 6–6 on aggregate on the away-goals ruling. Andy Walker got Celtic's other goal on a night in which they came within a whisker of qualifying.

Nine minutes from the end Celtic took the lead 5–3 to put themselves into a qualifying position but unbelievably they lost it in the final minute when Scepovic headed the goal that gave them overall victory.

Billy McNeill spoke for all when he said ruefully: 'That just sums up how cruel a game football can be when you climb three mountains and then throw yourself off the last one.'

Celtic's team was: Bonner, Grant, Rogan, Aitken, Elliott, Whyte, Galloway, McStay, Dziekanowski, Walker and Miller.
Subs: Andrews, McCahill, Fulton, Burns and Coyne.

23 April 1988

This was, and still is, an outstanding memory as it is a veritable oasis of glory in a barren desert of failure. It was, of course, the day when Billy McNeill returned in triumph to fulful all the wishes of the countless thousands of Celtic fans when the Centenary Championship was clinched in tremendous style.

A crowd, well in excess of 60,000 (many said more than 70,000), packed the ground in anticipation of one of the truly marvellous occasions for which Parkhead was renowned. They were not to be disappointed.

Dundee were the visitors and they were dealt an early indication of what was going to unfold before them when Chris Morris opened the scoring after only three minutes. Anton Rogan, that super-enthusiast who wore his Celtic heart on his sleeve, surged down the wing in typical cavalier fashion and Tom Carson did well to parry the Irishman's powerful cross. Unfortunately for the keeper, it landed straight at the feet of the dashing Morris who rifled it into the net to trigger off party-time.

If it had not been for the heroics of Carson the party would have been over even before the singing had reached full volume, for he produced wonder saves to deny Frank McAvennie three times and big Mick McCarthy twice. But even Tom was powerless to keep Celtic at bay for much longer and before the finish Andy Walker had buried two more past him to send the fans into raptures. The big-time was back and the fans were revelling in it.

The teams were:

CELTIC: Bonner, Morris, Rogan, Aitken, McCarthy, Whyte, Miller, McStay, McAvennie, Walker and Burns.
Subs: Stark and McGhee.
DUNDEE: Carson, Forsyth, Angus, Shannon, Smith, Saunders, Lawrence, Rafferty, Wright, Coyne and Campbell.
Subs: Frail and Harvey.

13 November 1968

The story of how Jimmy Johnstone almost single-handedly disman-tled Red Star Belgrade is a well-documented part of the Celtic folk-lore but it is always well worth the telling, especially for those youngsters who may have missed out first time round.

Aware of Jimmy's well-known fear of flying, that wily old character Jock Stein capitalised on it and the Yugoslavs were made to pay a terrible penalty. Big Jock took his mercurial genius aside and promised him if he delivered the goods in the first match of this European Cup second-round tie he would be excused having to travel to the return leg.

Jimmy was delighted. What a challenge! He could hardly wait to get at the poor Slavs and by the end of the night they were tortured and bewildered as the wee man turned on the style. It would have been easier for the visitors to have slapped the hand-cuffs on a ghost as Jinky tore them apart with his twisting and turning runs, leaving them with their tongues hanging out and their legs in knots.

Jimmy scored twice and laid on two of the others in a magnificent 5–1 display of all that is good about all-out, attractive and highly entertaining attacking play.

Like all good entertainers, he saved the best for the end as he ran on to a Bobby Murdoch pass and smashed the ball past bewildered keeper Durkovic. It was Murdoch who had set the pace with a goal in the third minute before Johnstone and Bobby Lennox made it three in the 47th and 50th minutes. Willie Wallace made it four in the 75th minute before Jimmy set the seal on a colossal performance with that spectacular strike in the 81st minute. Lazervic had netted for the Slavs in the 39th minute to give them hope but it soon disappeared when Jimmy turned on the magic.

It was arguably one of the finest ever displays from one man and the irony was to come later when Stein told Jimmy he was keen to keep to his word but added that the Slavs had pleaded with him to make sure Johnstone played in the return match. They said they wanted their own fans to see the real reason why their team had been so clinically destroyed. Jimmy declined with thanks.

The Celtic team that great night was: Fallon, Craig, Gemmell, Murdoch, McNeill, Brogan, Johnstone, Wallace, Chalmers, Lennox and Hughes.

17 December 1969

While Jimmy Johnstone obviously has very fond memories of the night he took Red Star apart he is not entirely convinced that was his finest performance ever. For he has very special memories, as I have, of an evening game on this night when former Rangers and Scotland winger Davy Wilson remained on the park to pass on his personal congratulations to Jinky and lift him up and show him off to the fans after Celtic had run amok, beating the Tannadice men 7–2. That night Celtic were truly out of this world and Jimmy was a megastar, providing the 26,000 fans with an unforgettable treat.

It was obvious from the kick-off that Jimmy was in the mood in what was a fantastic few days for the team, for they had taken four goals off St Johnstone three days earlier and hammered three more past Kilmarnock just three days after putting seven past Donald Mackay in United's goal. That made it 14 goals in three games in the space of a week.

Bertie Auld set the show in motion against United with a goal in the second minute and before half time Harry Hood, a Tommy

Gemmell penalty and John Hughes had made it four with United getting one through Mitchell. But Stein's Stunners were not finished yet and, just after the resumption, Wallace made it 6–1 with goals in the 46th and 52nd minutes. And even when Gordon got another for United, Murdoch went up the park minutes later to hammer home a seventh. And all of it was carried out with some intricate fine tuning and magnificently embroidered moves from Johnstone who was in unstoppable form.

The teams were:

CELTIC: Fallon, Hay, Gemmell, Murdoch, McNeill, Brogan, Johnstone, Hood, Wallace, Auld (Craig) and Hughes.
DUNDEE UNITED: Mackay, Rolland, J Cameron, Gillespie, Smith, Henry (K Cameron), Wilson, Reid, Gordon, Mitchell and Scott.

There were, of course, very many more excellent games played at Parkhead over the years but these, I hope you will agree, number among the most memorable.

COVENTRY CITY fans last week endorsed the long-term view held by Celtic, and supported by Celtic fans in a recent poll, that people enjoy standing at football matches. In a move that has surprised the all-seated stadium promoters, Coventry have decided to take out seats in a section of their stadium and made it into terracing. Talking of the club's fans, Coventry chairman John Paynton said: 'They like the warmth and banter of standing side by side on the terracing.'

Celtic View, 16 January 1985

CELTIC fans, it seems, just love bursting into print with poems in praise of their heroes and indeed all things associated with the club. The Jungle was an area which was to become immortalised in verse on more than one occasion. Here is one offering from Francis W.T. Cooper of Morris Place, Glasgow:

> St Peter's, St Paul's, the Taj Mahal,
> Have all won great renown.
> But to Celtic fans the greatest of all
> Was the Jungle they've just pulled down.

It wasn't a noble edifice
It was ugly and cast from tin
Yet thousands of fans spent happy hours,
The proof was the songs from within.

For an Orpheus Choir couldn't compete,
When the Bhoys decided to sing,
And the joyous shouts that greeted a goal,
Made all of its rafters ring.

What touchline artistes have raced its length,
Delaney, Collins and Weir,
Or Tully, or Murphy, or McAtee,
The memory brings many a tear.

Now like those stars it, too, has gone,
Leaving nought but an empty space,
But soon, like a Phoenix, there will emerge,
A building of beauty and grace.

And over the years the fans will revere
The new one just like the old,
And stirring tales of sweet success,
Will again and again be told.

Celtic View, 8 June 1966

I'LL never forget my one and only visit to the Jungle for I was there under orders from my husband so that I could take pictures and tell him in great detail about every minute of my stay there. The occasion was the triumphant homecoming of Jock Stein, Billy McNeill and the rest of the heroes who were later to be called the Lisbon Lions, and never was a name more appropriate. I have to say, even after all these years, that I went there rather reluctantly, never having been there before. But when I got there and saw the crowd I was soon caught up in the euphoria.

Where was my husband I hear you asking? He was still making his way home from Lisbon and, believe me, he was in no hurry as he was enjoying himself so much. He only stopped long enough to phone me and ask me to go to Parkhead on his behalf, so I was there by proxy, but it was brilliant. My only other visits to Parkhead, before and since then, have been to the stand. But this visit was really something special. The looks of pure adulation on the faces of the fans around me that night, as the players made their lap of honour, had to be seen to be believed. Grown men were weeping around me but they were crying tears of supreme happiness.

My only annoyance was that my husband had missed what was a glorious occasion, for my words, I am certain, did not adequately capture the situation. He did not complain, however, for he was still on Cloud Nine for weeks after his return from Lisbon. In conclusion, I'm sure Bob Hope would not be unduly bothered if I borrow his signature tune and say to Billy McNeill and his men – Thanks for the Memories.

Kathleen Reilly

I WAS as annoyed as everyone else when Mo Johnston snubbed Celtic to join Rangers, but when I thought about it and recalled how Alfie Conn came to us, it put it a wee bit more into perspective. After all, Alfie had played some great games for the Gers and had even punished us a couple of times but he had left them and gone to Spurs in between times. Anyway, he wasted no time in putting things right and showing the fans he would earn his keep at Parkhead by netting on his first appearance in the hoops at home. He had come on as a substitute at Aberdeen, just days after joining, but Celtic had lost that one 2–0. But a few days later he gave himself a good start with the fans, who took to him right away, when he scored his first goal. It was good enough to set Celtic on the road to a 2–1 win over Partick Thistle, but I must admit it was strange to see Alfie Conn and Johnny Doyle in the same team.

John McFarlane

Playing With Toy Motors in the Jungle

ONE of my earliest memories of going to the Jungle has nothing to do with football. I always thought it was a great wee place to play with my toy motor-cars! Mind you, in fairness, I was only a kid at the time and my dad, who always took me there, thought I was a wee pest as he had paid to get me in there to start my football education at the right place. After that, however, I started to go there regularly with my pals in the Sixties and had some great times, especially when the team picked up form and enjoyed great success both in domestic and European football. What I particularly enjoyed about the Jungle was the camaraderie that existed in there. The patter was fantastic and I suppose if I had known what I was going to do in my career, many years later, I would have paid more attention to the sayings and wit from that great place and the characters who gathered there. Later, I kept my options open, though, and went to matches at all the city grounds, but I'll never forget those early days in the Jungle where I had my own wee piece of earth to race my cars.

Dean Park, singer/comedian

I HAVE made only one visit to Celtic Park – but what a memorable experience it turned out to be. The 'All Stars' charity football team, of which I am coach, more in name than action, were invited to play against Dukla Pumpherston Sawmill and Tannery Football Club on the final night before the the Jungle was to be closed and turned into an all-seater area. As we walked out on to the pitch, the welcome given us was tremendous, especially from the Jungle fans. We were really proud to be there and the honour we felt at being at the park on such a memorable, and in part sad, occasion is beyond description. We were also made so welcome by the officials and everyone concerned that we really felt at home – even being allowed to don the famous green and white tracksuits.

Although the Jungle will never be the same again, I feel sure the spirit will remain because it is created by the fans themselves and I am sure there is nowhere in Britain where the enthusiasm and support could top that shown by the Celtic Park fans. They may now have to sing from a sitting position, but I am sure this will encourage them to sing even louder – just to prove that pulling down the standing area does not mean the 'death' of the Jungle. Hopefully, the 'All Stars' will be invited back to experience this for themselves.

Bill Tarmey, (Jack Duckworth) *Coronation Street*

I LOVED the Jungle in my younger days when I considered it was the only place to watch football at Parkhead, but I must admit I had one very worrying moment when, on reflection, I suppose I was lucky to escape without serious injury. It was just at the finish of the game and we were making our way out of the Jungle into Janefield Street when I tripped and fell. Within seconds there were dozens of bodies piling on top of me as the supporters crowded around the gate to get out. I honestly thought my time had come. I could barely breathe and could see nothing as I was underneath this mountain of bodies. Suddenly it all cleared and I was able to scramble shakily to my feet but, an hour later when I got home, I was still trembling with fright at the thought of what might have happened to me that day. I must say, though, it did not stop me going back to my favourite vantage spot – but now that I am a bit older the stand is the place for me.

Peter McGinn

SCRIPTWRITERS and budding comedians could have made their fortunes by going into the Jungle and just listening to the patter when the old place was in its heyday. Many years ago, a Mass was celebrated at Parkhead for a special occasion. It was in the early Fifties and the following week I was in the Jungle with my mate when Celtic were undergoing, shall we say, an uninspired afternoon. To be blunt, it was rotten. And the only good thing was the laughs we had from the many pattermen who stood in there. As a very dull game drew to a close, a fan near me said, 'I was at the Mass here last week and there was more movement from two of the statues that were carried in the procession than there has been all day from Haughney and Meechan.'

Pat Reilly

HERE is my team to 'conquer the world', selected from all the stars I played alongside: Alex Stepney (Manchester United), Danny

McGrain, Tommy Gemmell, Bobby Murdoch, Billy McNeill, Bobby Lennox, Jimmy Johnstone (all Celtic), Bryan Robson, Bobby Charlton, Denis Law and George Best (all Manchester United). And my substitute would be Ian Storey-Moore (Manchester United).

Lou Macari, the programme for his testimonial match between Manchester United and Celtic in May 1984

EMLYN HUGHES knew what he was talking about when he discussed the play of footballers in general and defenders in particular, having been over the course many times for Liverpool and England. So when he chose our own Tommy Gemmell for his best British side of a 20-year period it was a fine accolade for the big Celt.

Come to think of it, they had a bit in common for both Tommy and old 'Crazy Horse' were real swashbuckling types who loved to put the emphasis on entertainment. Tommy will forever be fondly remembered by Celtic fans for his great goals in the European Cup finals against Inter Milan in 1967 and Feyenoord in 1970. That was surely a rare achievement for a full-back, but then Tommy was more than just a defender. He was an all-round entertainer.

Paul Dickson, Dunfermline

WE all have our favourite players and I make no bones about mine. He is Roy Aitken – a man who gave his all for Celtic in more than 600 games and who retained his enthusiasm from his début at 16 until his departure some 15 years later.

I never fail to get annoyed when I hear so-called know-alls describe the big fellow as nothing more than a destroyer. For, to me, Roy had considerable skills, as he must surely have had to represent Scotland at almost every level from schoolboy, youth and under-21, before finally completing a half-century of caps in the senior ranks. You don't do that unless you can play a bit. Big Jock Stein, whose knowledge of the game and players was unrivalled, gave 'the Bear' his chance at the age of 16 and Roy went on to become a great Celt. He was a truly inspirational captain who never ever gave less than 100 per cent for the club he loved.

George Carroll, Port Glasgow

DURING the late Fifties to the early Seventies the Jungle was always full to the brim. So much so that when I was about 11 or 12 years old

I remember many times being lifted up by the surge of the crowd at the end of the game and being almost carried without my feet touching the ground until I had got across the road to the pavement at the wall of the cemetery.

James McCann

GOING to the same spot in the Jungle for every match made it more than just a game. It was a social outing. You could go to away games, as I did, and never meet anyone you knew. But as soon as you walked into the Jungle it was back to Paradise and old friends' reunion. I remember the usual crowd of us being at the game with Hamilton Accies in 1988. It was a hot summer's day and at half time we were four goals in the lead. We decided to relax a bit and take our tops off to do a bit of sunbathing. I saw one of my mates at work, who was an avid Accies fan, and Big Gordon never went anywhere without wearing his full-length mac. This day was no exception – regardless of the heat. We all started singing: 'Gordon, Gordon, take off your mac, Gordon, take off your mac.' Gordon listened to the Jungle chorus and took off his mac – you should have seen the grin on his face as the Jungle applauded him, but the Bhoys wiped that smile off his face with a 7–2 win.

Gary Scott, Liverpool

THERE have been some comedians on the park in my time of following the Celtic – with Tommy Gemmell right up there with the best. But I wonder how many of the younger element who follow the Celts these days know that a Gemmell lookalike, the real comedian-actor Danny Kaye (one of the finest funny men in the world), once came to see a Celtic game. Unfortunately, it was at Hampden and not Parkhead but the Jungle boys who were there loved him anyway. I was there as a wee boy with my father and I have only a very faint recollection of him being there. In fact, being honest, I didn't even know who he was, but I was reminded many times in growing up that I was there when Danny was in Glasgow and he came to the game to kick-off before a Charity Cup final with Rangers in 1950.

Robert Kilpatrick, Milngavie

CHAPTER TWELVE

The Day Charlie 'Nicked' a Jersey

CHARLIE NICHOLAS at least had the good grace to blush when he recalled how he once borrowed or, to use his own phrase, 'nicked' a strip to wear to the Jungle to support Celtic in a vital match with Rangers. And he confesses he has not a shred of remorse about the dastardly deed but even now he admits to a shudder of fear when he thinks of the risks he took and how he could have been caught by the dreaded custodian of the jerseys – Neilly Mochan. With his eyes twinkling like a mischievous schoolboy, Charlie recalls the day of that great laundry-room robbery. And the memory could not be more vivid if it happened yesterday, rather than many years ago.

'It was on 21 May 1979,' says Charlie, 'and I can pinpoint the jersey hi-jacking almost to the minute. How could I ever forget it. I was terrified Neilly would come in and catch us and we'd have been for the high jump. I'd only been on the groundstaff a couple of months and had graduated to there from my usual place in the Jungle, which to me was the only place to watch the game. I always used to go there with my pals when I wasn't playing for the school team or boys club. Anyway, this day we were all up to high doh for it was the night of the title-winning clash with Rangers. But don't rush me, I want to tell you how it happened.

'As I say I was on ground staff duty with Danny Crainie and Willie McStay, Paul's elder brother, and the three of us and Neilly were the only ones there during the day. Our job was to clear out the dressing-rooms and help Neilly get the kit ready for the players for that night's game. About two o'clock Neilly told us we could go but to be back sharp at 6 p.m. Now none of us had a car and I lived in Maryhill, Danny in Croy and Willie in Larkhall, so we decided to go into the town for a bite to eat to help pass the time. When we headed back to the Park we got everything in order and, when Neilly was having a cup of tea, which he liked doing before the big games, we saw our chance. We slipped into the laundry-room, got three jerseys and put them on under our clothes and sloped off round to the Jungle half an hour before kick-off. When we got in there among the fans we slipped off the jackets to reveal the strips. Talk about being ten feet tall! We were chuffed to bits. It was an unforgettable feeling, wearing the real strip while roaring on the lads.

'And what a night it was. There was a crowd of over 50,000 and big Roy Aitken, George McCluskey, a Colin Jackson own goal and a belter from Murdo MacLeod gave us a 4–2 win. The Celtic punters went bananas. The title was won, Rangers were beaten and it had all happened on home territory. But when the lads were doing their well-earned lap of honour, which took them right past us in the Jungle, we suddenly realised we were bang in trouble if we didn't get the jerseys back before Neilly found out. Believe me, that would have been a fate worse than death – we would have been cleaning those dressing-rooms until we were old men. Tommy Burns was the one with the eagle eyes who spotted us in the Jungle near the Celtic End and a couple of days later, when the strips were safely back in place, he asked if we had nicked them from the laundry room. What could we say? We had to own up and take our punishment but, thankfully, the victory had taken the sting out of Neilly and we escaped with a telling-off. What a difference a result like that win over Rangers can make, eh?'

That is only one of many great memories Charlie has of the place where he grew up amid the great all-singing, all-dancing days and nights of his youth – spent supporting his beloved Celtic. "I love every part of the place," says Charlie, 'but the Jungle was always that wee bit more special to me for it is the place I would have been standing in all those years if I had never had the good fortune to be a Celtic player. I never tire of thinking about the great games we played there and of the marvellous feeling of knowing every single man, woman and child in there was willing you on to victory. The sight of those fans in the Jungle was the first thing that hit you when you ran out of the tunnel. The sound of that massed choir singing 'You'll Never Walk Alone' while holding their scarves at arms length above their heads – it was one of the greatest sights in football and

I'm only glad to have witnessed it first hand, both as a player and fan. It was and is a privilege to have been part of it.'

'I could go on all night about great games, but one I'll never forget is my first game against Rangers at Celtic Park, when I scored twice. That was in February 1981 and we won 3–1, with big Roy Aitken getting our other goal. That was an unbelievable experience for me and the fans in the Jungle had a lot to do with it. I was a wee kid then and when I scored that first goal I went a bit crazy. I ran to the Jungle like somebody demented. The fans were chanting my name and it was a dream come true. Usually, you are only aware of a sea of faces and a mass of colour in the crowd but that time I could see individual faces vividly and it stuck with me as I saw the joy on their faces and the effect that goal had. It brought home to me just what it meant to be a Celtic supporter and how it felt to be a goal up against your greatest rivals. That is a feeling that will live with me forever. The fans in the Jungle have been brilliant to me during my entire career. They are a genuine inspiration and you honestly feel their incredible backing just when you run out on to the park.

'The Jungle was always my place and, although I realise you must move with the times, I was saddened when the seats went in there. I know it's daft but I would have preferred if they had seated the ends first and left the Jungle to last. Still it's done now and as long as we get support not just from that part of the ground but also from the rest, and let's face it they have their traditions too, I'll be a happy man.'

Charlie is one of very few players who got the chance to play to two of the best-known and most heavily congested areas of football stadia – the Jungle and the North Bank at Arsenal. Kenny Dalglish was another, of course, when he left Celtic to become an idol of the Kop at Liverpool. And both were given heroes' receptions by their new-found fan clubs. Charlie tells of his love for both supporters' terracings in *The End*, the story of the 80-year history of the North Bank at Highbury. He recalls he never had an ego problem believing fantasies about himself: 'I've got my own beliefs and I'm very easily satisfied. My being satisfied is giving a bit of entertainment when I'm playing on a Saturday, or watching a bit of entertainment on a Saturday from great players I've played with at Arsenal and Celtic. My father used to take me to Parkhead and sit me on a barrier when I was just six or seven and I was very fortunate because I watched the Lisbon Lions there. I saw greatness and success plus entertainment. Between the ages of seven and 15 it was a dream for me. I mean I saw Kenny Dalglish before he left Celtic; I once bumped into him and I was terrified to ask him for his autograph. I used to see all the Celtic people at functions and I'd never ask for their autographs. I was petrified of the people; I was in awe of them. Even now, I mean, Dalglish and I get on very well but I'm still in awe of him.

'My first game with Arsenal I was aware of a new crowd. I suddenly started feeling pressure, to be honest, as we were going down the tunnel. But when the game started I thought "hang on". I felt I hadn't really moved clubs. I had the same affection there I had got at Celtic and for that alone I am ever so grateful. You know it breaks you, leaving a club, especially for me at Celtic and Arsenal. I was aware of how the crowd at Celtic felt when I left, because I was on the terraces when Dalglish left and he was my hero. The reaction when he left was one of numbness.' Charlie goes on: 'I was dreading the Paul Davis testimonial as by that time I had left Arsenal and, after Aberdeen, had gone back to Celtic. And I didn't know how I'd be received by the punters on the North Bank. I didn't get much feedback when I ran out but I clapped them and they responded. Gradually, they were really giving it strong to me and at the end of the night I went over and gave them my Celtic jersey. At that time a lot of Celtic fans who drank in my pub were there and they couldn't believe the reception I got having left a big club like that.'

One Arsenal fan, who obviously though a lot of Charlie, made his feelings crystal clear in the book. Stewart O'Brien said: 'Charlie had never got a chance to say goodbye to the Arsenal fans until that Paul Davis testimonial when he came back with Celtic. At the end of the game, he takes his shirt off and where did he run to? He comes to the North Bank and throws his shirt into the crowd. The whole place just went up. Born is the King of Highbury. Charlie, Charlie.'

Jinky 'Puts the Boot' into the Jungle

JIMMY JOHNSTONE will never ever forget the night he 'put the boot into the Jungle fans' – in the nicest possible way, of course. He tells the story well all these years later as, eyes gleaming, he turns back the years.

He says: 'It was just one of those things, a real spontaneous gesture 'cos I couldn't think of how else to repay those fantastic supporters. We were playing a real star-studded Manchester United team in what was a testimonial for my great pal Bobby Lennox and myself. I had been with Sheffield United but my heart was still with Celtic, even though I had been given a free transfer. Anyway, I was told I was getting a testimonial along with Lemon (Lennox) and for the three weeks before it I trained morning, noon and night to get myself in the best possible shape. It was a wee bit of pride, I suppose, but I felt I owed it to them and to myself to look the part.

'I'll never forget it, the night was 17 May 1976 and I was nervous, really nervous. I had punished myself to get into condition but I was frightened I would let anyone down. Anyway, we got to Parkhead and I was like a wee schoolboy getting a trial with my favourite team. I had seen a lot and done a lot over the years, but somehow this was different. The night kicked off with my big pal Billy Connolly refereeing an Old Crocks game and the Big Yin noised up the fans in the Jungle by wearing a Rangers scarf.

'While that was going on out there I was working myself into a wee knot in the dressing-room. The two teams lined up in a circle and applauded me and Bobby. The fans' reception, from a staggering crowd of 50,000 on a soaking-wet night, was fantastic. Every time Bobby or myself touched the ball the supporters went wild. It was incredible stuff and I was loving every minute of it by then. Kenny Dalglish was fantastic that night, grabbing a hat-trick, and wee Bobby got the other one as we won 4–0. But it was after that it all got to me as Bobby and I did a lap of honour. I had a huge lump in my throat and was blinded by tears as we ran to the Jungle. Now, as you know, the Jungle was always my favourite spot. I loved them and, thankfully, they loved me. I thought, "How can I repay them on my last game for them?" The answer came in a flash: I threw one of my boots in and then ran along the line to another spot and chucked the other one in there. I thought, "That'll keep two fans happy." I was going to throw in my jersey, too, but I felt that my boots would be an even more special souvenir. It was spontaneous and the punters loved it. Well, two of them did anyway. Now I know this is hard to believe but later, when I was playing back in my roots with Blantyre Celtic, a fan came up and said to me, "I've got one of your boots." He had as well, and had brought it along to show me. It was mine all right – I recognised it as the one with the stud missing.'

Jimmy Johnstone is one of that special breed of entertainers whose name is instantly recognised and summed up in one word. In his case it is *Jinky* – and no one-word description was ever more appropriate. The marvellously talented little winger, whose trademarks were his consummate ball skills and his curly red hair, belongs to the ranks of top-quality stars who achieved such fame. Who ever called Francis Albert anything other than Sinatra? Elvis could only be one man, Pavarotti another, and Swing King Basie was out on his own as a one-man band. And on the football pitch Jinky ranked in stature alongside Stein, Baxter, Law and Best. Even megastars such as Pele, Cruyff and Puskas knew and applauded the twisting and tormenting turns of the little maestro who graced the full length of that area in front of the Jungle for 14 years.

But lionised as he was by the Parkhead faithful, Jimmy modestly admits he was nothing without his audience of adoring fans in what he calls 'my place'. The youngest of five children Jimmy was born on 15 September 1944 in Viewpark, Lanarkshire and was destined for stardom from that day onwards. Modelling himself on the great Stanley Matthews, the diminutive one, with a temper to match his red hair, graduated through the Parkhead ranks from ballboy to world superstar. But he never forgot his roots. And if he had never made it as a player, whose skills rivalled the Parkhead pylons in lighting up the skies on big European nights, Jimmy would have been found in the Jungle among the scarves, banners, pies and bovril merchants.

Looking back on a career which saw him score 115 goals in more than 450 games for his beloved Celts, Jimmy has few regrets. One he refuses to dwell on, however, is the fact that his highly individual performances were never seen in a World Cup finals series. But Jinky gets just as much fun, if not more, in recalling his glory days strutting his stuff before his vast army of followers – even if it did constantly get him in trouble with his great mentor Jock Stein. Rarely included in team talks by Stein, who knew it would be easier to slip the handcuffs on a ghost than to tie Jinky down, the wee man nevertheless fell foul of the Big Man for his cantrips down the wing. His face positively glows as he recalls: 'The Big Man knew how I loved to play up to the fans in the Jungle and would cross the park to show off to them at every opportunity.' With that impish grin, reminiscent of the wayward schoolboy, Jimmy says: 'To be honest, the Big Man put up with a lot from me but sometimes he would crack up when I was doing the business on the Jungle side when I would have been better off on the stand side. I've lost count of the times he would send Neilly Mochan haring round the track to tell me to cut out the nonsense and get back to my beat on the other side.

I'd say to Neilly, "Turn it up, gie the boys a turn. They've paid their money and I want to turn it on for them." It was always in my mind to try my best to entertain them. They were the ones who paid their way in, regardless of anything else. It must have been difficult for many of them, financially speaking, and I felt I owed them something in return. I loved kicking down the stand side in the first half for it meant I would be in front of the Jungle for the second and that sometimes led to a real finale. But the Big Man used to crack up at me and even though I was terrified of him, I couldn't stop myself nipping over to play up to the Jungle.' He adds: 'They were my people. I identified closely with them. They were the first people who caught your eye when you ran out the tunnel and they were the last to cheer you off the park if you had done the business for them. I always felt a great response from them. Hairs used to stand up on the back of my neck before I went out to play in front of those fans. I did the business for them.

'I know when people talk of the great games I played, the one that crops up most is the European Cup tie with Red Star Belgrade in November 1968. That is the one where the Big Man promised me I wouldn't have to make the return trip because of my fear of flying. But the condition was that I did the business in the first leg and I played my part with two goals in a 5–1 victory. That was a great game, but I don't think it was my all-time best.

'I was lucky enough to turn it on a few times and the one that sticks out in my memory is a 7–2 win over Dundee United at Parkhead in December 1969. The lads in the Jungle that night were unbelievable and we responded in style. It poured rain all through the game but the fans never stopped their singing and encouragement and, believe me, they had plenty to sing about that night. We gave them the lot. It was all done in our own style with non-stop attacks. We were at United's throats all the time and, to be honest, they played their part, too, in coming back at us. But at that time we always knew if a team scored a couple against us we would lift the pace and go one better. We proved it that night and the fans in the Jungle lapped it up as we gave them a night to remember.

'The play flowed non-stop and it was exciting stuff all the way. What made it even better was that we got the goals to match and the Jungle fans went wild. I would class that as one of our best ever performances and, at the risk of blowing my own trumpet, it was one of those nights when I could do no wrong. I gave them everything I had and I will never forget the end of it all when wee Davy

Wilson, who had gone to Tannadice from Rangers, waited for me at the end and threw his arms round me and led me to the Jungle area to let the fans give me an extra-special reception that will live with me all of my life. Coming from a player who was himself an international star, that was really something to be appreciated. And the guys and lassies in the Jungle took a shine to him for that one thoughtful gesture. Let's face it, that game was a quarter of a century ago, but I can recall it and the fans' response as though it was last week.'

He adds: 'I know how fans like to read about these occasions so for the record our goals came from Wispy Wallace, who got two, Harry Hood, Bobby Murdoch, Bertie Auld and John Hughes, who all got singles, and big Tam Gemmell blasted in one of his unstoppable penalties. I have had many games I was proud to have taken part in and that stands up there alongside all of them. And we couldn't have done it without the fans in the Jungle. They were immense that night – but what's new about that? Celtic fans were, to me at any rate, the greatest in the world and that wee stretch in the Jungle summed them up for me. They were simply the best.'

Locked in – Before the Game

FRANK MCGARVEY swears he is only slightly exaggerating with his claim that he could have beaten Linford Christie in a short sprint at Parkhead on 2 April 1980. The reason? He had just scored his first goal for Celtic against Rangers and it proved to be the winner. And the memory of this goal, only one of more than 100 he netted for Celtic, is indelibly inscribed into Frank's brain. 'I still get a great glow of pride when I think back to that goal for, although I had opened my account for Celtic against Hibs in the previous match, this was my first against Rangers and it means so much to me. My immediate thought was to run to the Jungle, as that was where I had stood on countless occasions as a Celtic fan long before I ever dreamed of playing for them.'

This time, however, he was definitely over the top in his estimation as he declares: 'I think I covered about 40 yards in two seconds.' He continues: 'That was undoubtedly the highlight of my career at Parkhead and it is one moment I will never, ever forget. There were plenty more great days and I enjoyed them all but, because I was a fan as well as a player, it is the games with Rangers plus the big European nights that stick out for me. I was lucky to have played for Celtic at a good time and figured in only one losing game against Rangers at Parkhead and that was the time when Alex Miller scored in the final minute. It was a fabulous strike but I still kid Alex on about it being just a winder at the ball. He swears, however, that not only did he mean it but that it was *not* the best goal he ever scored. I'd like to have seen the others!'

He adds: 'But that first game against Rangers was fantastic for me as it looked as though we were going to have to settle for a draw. I thought I had cracked it earlier, but Peter McCloy pulled off a marvellous save from my header to keep the scoreline blank. Then, with only five minutes to go, Roy Aitken crossed and I dived to head the ball into the net. I admit I almost went wild with delight. I had played only three games for Celtic before this one and it was a real dream come true for me to score that winner in my first Old Firm match. But if I thought I enjoyed it, the feeling was certainly shared by the packed Jungle. They went bananas! They were still cheering and roaring their heads off when the final whistle sounded and it was music to my ears to hear them chant my name.

'That goal alone made me forget my nightmare year at Liverpool, when I had gone south with such high hopes from St Mirren, only to fail to get a chance to show what I could do for the first team. When Billy McNeill came in for me I leapt at the chance to join Celtic and I never regretted it. Playing before those fans in the Jungle was always a dream of mine, especially when I was standing in there with them, cheering on the lads. I have always maintained the Jungle fans were not only the most loyal but also the most knowledgeable. The Jungle was always accepted as the real heart of the Celtic support and I'll never tire of watching videos showing that packed area as a mass of green and white with scarves raised above their heads, swaying to the tune of one of their many songs.

'I am sure that sight must have put the fear of death into many a team at Parkhead, especially foreigners on European duty. Celtic fans adored those big nights in Europe and one I'll never forget was the time we came back from Lisbon 2–0 down to Sporting and the

Jungle that night was absolutely amazing. We sensed it was going to be one of the really good nights when we went out for the warm-up. The fans were already in full voice and the players got caught up in the excitement.

'The Sporting players did not know what hit them that night. We had been terrible over there and were lucky to get away only two goals down. They came here thinking they were on their holidays and couldn't possibly lose. We had other thoughts and they must have felt as though they were facing 11 madmen the way we tore into them from the start. Our manager, Davie Hay, had literally to bar the door before kick-off, so desperate were we to get out and get started. Tommy Burns gave us the lead and just before half time Tom McAdam and Brian McClair put us in front on aggregate. The Portuguese did not know what had hit them and before the finish we had swept them aside with two more goals from Murdo MacLeod and myself. Unfortunately, in the next round, after a creditable no-scoring draw against Nottingham Forest down there, we went out, beaten 2–1 at Parkhead.'

There were other great European nights for Frank at Parkhead and although he did not start against Italian giants Juventus – Liam Brady and all – he played in the second match in Turin. And another tie which holds special memories is the 4–3 aggregate defeat of Ajax of Amsterdam.

'The Jungle gave us their all in that first match against Johan Cruyff and his mates at Parkhead when Charlie Nicholas and I scored our two goals in a 2–2 draw. We thought we had blown it then but I honestly thought we had transported the entire Jungle to Holland when George McCluskey scored two minutes from time to give us a 2–1 win over there.'

McGarvey became the first player to score a century of Premier League goals when he netted a hat-trick for Celtic against his old buddies St Mirren in November 1984. But his Celtic career came to a shocking end when he was transferred back to Saints just days after scoring the winner against Dundee United in the Scottish Cup final. Ironically, it was an action replay of that first goal he scored against Rangers when he dived to head home an Aitken cross. Despite the timing of his departure, Frank has too many happy memories and too much love for the club to dwell on any thoughts of bitterness. 'That's in the past and, in any case, my great memories more than compensate for anything else,' says Frank.

Kenny's Neighbour in the Jungle

KENNY DALGLISH paraded his unique talents before his massed army of fans in the Jungle on very many occasions during his ten years with Celtic. He has great memories of Old Firm clashes and big European matches but the one that sticks out most in his mind is his début against Raith Rovers on 4 October 1969. The reason for that is not because Celtic won 7–1, although obviously that delighted him, but he will never forget running across to the Jungle to take a throw-in and picking out the unmistakable face of a near-neighbour yelling support for him. Kenny recalls: 'It's amazing when you think the Jungle was packed to capacity with thousands of Celtic fans roaring us on and yet the one face that stood out for me was a neighbour who stayed just across the road from my parents' house. He was cheering and roaring support for me and I thought that was terrific.'

The fan certainly got full value for money that day as Celtic beat the Fifers 7–1 with the goals coming from Bobby Lennox and Jimmy Johnstone, who got two each, Tommy Callaghan, John Hughes and Willie Wallace. Jock Stein knew what he was doing when he launched Kenny's career alongside seven of the men who became immortalised as the Lisbon Lions.

The Celtic team on that début day for the 18-year-old Dalglish was Simpson, Hay and Gemmell, Dalglish, McNeill and Clark, Johnstone, Lennox, Wallace, Callaghan and Hughes. Harry Hood was on the bench.

Kenny recalls: 'That was memorable, but to be honest there were many more great days and nights. Old Firm matches were magic when the Jungle came into its own. European nights were brilliant with the floodlights on and the fans roaring us on. The fans in the Jungle were really fantastic and their encouragement to the young players is legendary. I was lucky enough to play in a reserve side that had quality all the way through it, with such class players as George Connelly, Davie Hay, Lou Macari and Victor Davidson.' They were well-named the Quality Street Gang and Kenny says it was a pleasure to play with them.

'I'll always remember my first ever game before the Jungle. It was an Old Firm reserve cup final and we won. You would have thought it was the senior team from the reception we got from those fans. That level of support was terrific and, happily, it stayed with me all the time I was at Parkhead.

'One thing that made the Jungle so special, and so different, is that it ran the whole length of the park so you were guaranteed support all the way along the pitch. Other standing areas such as the Kop, which was to become so familiar and so supportive to me, made up only one side of the ground. I know every single player in my time had a special feeling for the Jungle and big Yogi Hughes certainly falls into that category. He just loved playing down the Jungle side of the park,' says Kenny. He adds laughingly: 'Mind you another reason for that was because it took him away from the sound of Jock Stein's voice. And the big man, when at full throttle, could make more noise than the Jungle itself.'

Dalglish went on to become a Celtic, Liverpool and Scotland legend as a player, being the only man to score a century of goals on both sides of the border. On hanging up his boots, the former idol of the Jungle also wrote his name into the record books as a manager to rank alongside the very best.

IT was lashing as my pal and I were heading to Hampden for the Scottish Cup final with Aberdeen in 1967 so, as we went to Central station to catch the train to Mount Florida, we decided to treat ourselves to a new bunnet. As Chic Murray would have said, 'it was one each you understand'. All went well and we got to the famous slopes but during the game, which Celtic won 2–0 by the way with two goals from Willie Wallace, there were other spectators present, other than those with their feet on the terracing. They were the Glasgow pigeons. Big, fat and overfed they were and they were right up there above us. At least they were until one dropped a message – right on my new bunnet.

There were 126,102 fans there that day and that b...... pigeon had to pick on my new bunnet. Not even my mate's, mind you, just mine. Ruined it was. I don't know what had been in that bird's diet but it was powerful stuff as it burned a hole right through my new headgear. 'Never mind,' said my pal, 'they say that's good luck.' Well it might have been at that for, after all, we did win the Cup didn't we?

Arthur

George Connelly's Warm-Up Exhibition

TRAGEDY is much too strong a word ever to be associated with sport – with the obvious exceptions of the Rangers disaster, when 66 fans died, and a similar catastrophe which happened at Hillsborough. But you can substitute another, lesser, adjective to describe the downfall of George Connelly and the feeling would still be the same. To me, Big George was a superb talent. He had ability and a real calm approach to the game as he proved on countless occasions.

Two situations concerning George's career at Parkhead stand out for me. How about his display of ball control and, to use a slang word, 'bottle' when just a kid in 1966. He was on the groundstaff at Parkhead at the time and used to amaze the senior players with his skill in the old-fashioned 'keepy-uppy' style. Jock Stein, never a man to ignore the chance of a wee bit of something different to entertain the fans, got the big lad to do his stuff in front of the 64,000 fans at Parkhead for the European Cup Winners Cup quarter-final with Dynamo Kiev in January 1966. It was only part of the warm-up entertainment but, with respect to Celtic's 3–0 victory that night, it outshone the game. The memory of that has outlasted many an important game. Jimmy Johnstone got one and Bobby Murdoch the other two goals that night, but the big Fifer was the star for the fans. George said later he hadn't felt nervous at all and had managed about ten minutes without dropping the ball. The big shy lad played it down but the crowd lapped it up. It was a brilliant exhibition of control and one I'll never forget.

The other occasion was four years later when George was established in the side and renowned for his brilliant use of the long, accurate ball to the forwards. My memory is of George at Leeds United's Elland Road ground in the European Cup semi-final first leg in 1970. The late Don Revie's white arrows were supposed to sweep Celtic out of the game in this original version of the 'Battle of Britain' but an early strike by the big lad ensured that this was not going to be the case and Celtic came home with a great advantage. The return was taken to Hampden with the result that it created a European Cup record attendance of 136,505 – and that was only the official version.

Yet, despite his ability to handle that sort of pressure, big George eventually quit the game prematurely. His skill was such that he was voted Player of the Year by the Scottish Football Writers' Association in 1973; but the following year he left Parkhead for good at the age of 24, saying he could not take the pressure any more. Now I know that it's not a tragedy in the real sense of the word but it was still a terrible waste of talent.

Pat Connolly, East Kilbride

IT did not take Polish international star striker Jacki Dziekanowski long to master the good old Glasgow phrase for being, shall we say, a shade disappointed. 'I'm sick,' was his short but highly appropriate description of his feelings on the night he scored four goals only to see Celtic tumble out of the European Cup Winners Cup, beaten on the away-goals rule by Partizan Belgrade.

His two-word summing-up must have been repeated thousands of times all over the country by Celtic fans that night in September 1989. And it was no great consolation to the 49,500 fans there to know they had just witnessed one of the greatest nights of excitement seen in a European cup-tie for many years.

The Yugoslavian Cup-holders had come to Parkhead with only the slight cushion of a 2–1 win at home with Euro-expert Mike Galloway having thrown Celtic a lifeline in the first tie. Little did they know of the drama in store, especially after they increased their lead to two goals after only eight minutes at Parkhead.

But they had reckoned without the mercurial Jacki, who took it upon himself to launch a one-man crusade. Two goals by the Polish striker made it 3–3 but when the visitors scored again it looked all over bar the shouting with those two away goals. Again, Jacki came to the rescue, driving home spectacularly from a pass by his pal Roy Aitken to make it 4–4. Still the Parkhead fans and players alike suffered a jangiing of the nerves as more drama unfolded with the visitors again going ahead at 5–4 but, incredibly, it was still not over as Andy Walker got in on Jacki's one-man show by shooting powerfully home to make it all square on a 5–5 aggregate.

Then, with emotions running high, Dziekanowski completed what had been a fabulous personal showing by putting Celtic ahead for the first time nine minutes from the end. Surely now the lads will hold out, we all thought. Sadly, we were wrong. In the final minute fate intervened when a Slav headed past Bonner to make it 5–4 for Celtic but 6–6 on aggregate.

All of the fans headed, shell-shocked, for the exits. And I recall telling my mate, who was distraught, that we had witnessed one of the most exciting nights ever in Europe. 'So what,' said he, 'we are out in the first round.' And, in honesty, although it had been a great night, those few words, like Jacki's, summed it up perfectly.

John Reilly

AT a loose end one day, I strolled into Celtic Park to pass the time and was enjoying myself leaning on a crush barrier in the Jungle watching four men (I think they were OAPs) spreading soil on the playing pitch. It turned out they were doing odd jobs around the place, and there are always plenty of those to be done at a football ground. This day their job was spreading this fine soil which was piled up at the edge of the touchline. I once had a wee spell working with the Parks Department in Glasgow and, although I would not consider myself an expert, I knew a bit about greenkeeping. I soon found out the four men also knew their business.

But as I watched I saw a familiar figure appear from the players' tunnel. I recognised the walk from the slight limp and realised immediately it was the Great Man himself, Jock Stein. I was all agog wondering what he was going to do but he strolled up to the men and right away got hold of a spare spade and slid it into the heap of earth. Being a working man all of my life, with many years spent on the tools in the shipyards, I am very critical of people using equipment of any sort. When I see actors on television or films pretending to work I am always scornful of their efforts; some of their efforts at using hammers or pinch bars are laughable. You would think they would pay someone to show them how to use tools properly before filming.

So, I was looking for faults with Big Jock, but there were none to be seen. He swung the loaded spade in an arc in expert fashion, giving it the necessary flick as the soil left the spade to send it in an even spray over the grass. I shouldn't have been surprised, of course, as the Big Man had been a miner in his early days and used the spade to the manner born. Anyway, I thought it was a nice gesture by Mr Stein to be on such friendly terms with the men that he would even assist them in their work. I'm glad I was there to see it.

James Canovan, Parkhead

CHAPTER THIRTEEN

From Auchenshuggle to Argentina – Via Tramcar and Jet Plane

THE theme of the Jungle first registered with me 50-odd years ago as a boy in Dalmuir West when I used to travel to Parkhead to worship my boyhood heroes – Delaney, McDonald, Crum, Divers and Murphy. I had to make a long tramcar journey from Dalmuir West terminus, just along from my home in Burns Street, on the quaintly named Auchenshuggle tram which took me straight to the Parkhead door. It was a 'penny special' journey and it took an age to cover the iron miles to Paradise but I passed the time on the trip by counting the number of pawn shops from Dalmuir to Bridgeton Cross – the number 51 comes to mind. This exercise helped me to pass the time on the shoogly journey and also assisted me with my arithmetic.

It was important for me to get to the Jungle early, in order to get as near the wall that divided me from my heroes as possible. You could hear their breathing, see the beads of sweat, witness their joy, share their anguish. We could rejoice with them, chide them, humour them and, most important of all, lift them. That was the real character of the Jungle.

The Jungle was packed with a real cross-section of the population. Most were products of Scotland's heavy industries of the time – dockers, riveters, welders, hauders-on. There were labourers from Clyde Shipbuilders, steelworkers and miners from Lanarkshire, building and construction workers and the famous 'McAlpine Fusiliers' – the Irish navvies. The one thing they had in common was that they were there to support their beloved Glasgow Celtic. And the bond between the players and the fans had to be seen to be believed.

From the Jungle we gazed across at the stand and wondered who were the gentry who sat there in such style. We felt they were too far from the players and the action. We were right there beside them – and we were also right beside the referees. We knew them. How we knew them! We advised them on their eyesight, sometimes we doubted their parentage. We could tell how they shook hands with the captains. We would say: 'That big toe-rag has just worked the grip – we've nae chance the day, just wait and see.' Some of the Jungle fans were miles ahead of their time. The comments made in there were typical West of Scotland humour, delivered with style, and that was what made the Jungle the Jungle.

After National Service with the RAF I was demobbed to find the 'penny special' had been replaced by the supporters' bus and two shillings a week (ten pence) took the Jungleites to far-off places such as Aberdeen, Dundee, Stirling, Dunfermline, Motherwell, and we sang our way round Scotland. Our bus, the Emerald supporters club from Whitecrook, left from outside the world-famous John Brown's shipyard in Clydebank. There was a strong link between Celtic and the yard as Glen Daly, a former shipyard worker, recorded the Celtic song which became our anthem.

One of the football greats who loved the Jungle as much as we loved him was Charles Patrick Tully. And many a time he had words with us before, after and sometimes even during games. That was the advantage of the wall. You could have a wee blether with the players over it. At the time, little did I realise how radically things would change with the arrival of Jock Stein and, I am proud to say, my wife, Kathleen, and I played major roles in that transformation.

In April 1966 the sun shone on us when we won the Championship and entry into the European Cup. The furthest we had travelled before that was to Aberdeen and the like, but now our passports were to be stamped with such place names as Amsterdam, Copenhagen, Malta, Nantes, Milan, Florence, Basle, Lisbon, Budapest, Buenos Aires and Montevideo. We formed a travel club within our travel company, Holiday Enterprises, and I remember phoning Jungle and stand men alike, asking did they fancy following the Bhoys? Tony Queen, the Glasgow bookmaker and a great pal of Jock Stein's, was first to book and it was amazing how the word travelled after that. We stayed at the Royals, the Intercontinentals, the Hiltons and the like – changed days again for a wee boy from the Jungle. Our longest ever trip was to South America and we had 'regulars' such as Bill and Jean Longmore who never missed a flight. Great days and we loved them all, living up to the best slogan of all, 'We shall all be moved'.

Jim McGinley

WILLIE O'NEILL may not be the best known Celtic full-back but he was a more than competent defender who was unlucky to be at Parkhead at the same time as Tommy Gemmell. But Willie has one claim to fame that no one can take away from him. He is in the record books as Celtic's first ever official substitute, coming on to replace Jimmy Johnstone in a League Cup match against St Mirren in September 1966. And big George Connelly also wrote his name into the records by becoming the first substitute used by a British club in the final of the European Cup. Big George came on for Bertie Auld against Feyenoord in the San Siro Stadium in Milan.

Phil O'Brien, Motherwell

DO you remember the signature tune that introduced the old television programme *Z Cars*? I do, and it almost caused problems the first time I went into the Jungle at Parkhead. The programme was very popular at the time and the record of the theme music was played before the game. But when the fans in the Jungle heard it over the Tannoy they went bananas and started shouting for it to be stopped. The reason? They thought it was an Orange tune and, when you think about it, I suppose there is a similarity. Anyway, the music played on and the team won, although for the life of me I can't remember who we were playing that day. Only the reaction to the tune stands out in my memory.

John McDermott

Kelly Kept the Flag Flying

THE late Sir Robert Kelly carved his name in the history books as a top legislator and as the man who gave his name to the 'Kelly Kids', who were later welded into such a formidable side by the great Jock Stein. But I am old enough to remember him for another very important reason – he was the man who kept the Eire flag flying proudly on the mast above the Jungle about 40 years ago. Celtic had been involved in several clashes with the SFA at that time, if my memory serves me right. There had been supporter trouble and the whole business was discussed by the City Fathers in George Square. They came up with several ideas for discussion by the football authorities and one was that Celtic and Rangers should stop displaying flags which might incite trouble.

Celtic took this as a reference to the Republican flag, which at that time flew over the Jungle. There was a lot of talk about it and the SFA ruled that Celtic had to stop displaying any flag that had no association with the country or the sport. Bob Kelly addressed the full meeting of the SFA and defended the right of the club to fly the flag as a reminder of the association the club had with its Irish founders. All sorts of threats were made, including one that promised the closure of the ground if there was any further trouble. Celtic were under constant pressure from the SFA but Bob Kelly withstood it all and emerged triumphant.

Charlie Donnelly

JOCK STEIN was, without doubt, a magnificent manager with a record that stands the utmost scrutiny, but even the big man could not wave a magic wand to guarantee instant success. Mind you, it looked as though he had this quality when he arrived back at Parkhead as manager in March 1965 after spells with Dunfermline and Hibs. I was at his first game in charge when Celtic beat Airdrie 6–0 at Broomfield, with Bertie Auld scoring five goals and big John Hughes the other. Two of Bertie's goals were from the penalty spot but it was still an exciting start to Stein's career as Parkhead boss. This was it, we all thought, the Big Man is back to lead us to greater glory than we ever imagined. He did. But it did not happen right away for in the very next match, just three days later, Celtic were brought down to earth with a bump when St Johnstone beat us 1–0 at Parkhead. Still, it all came good in the end and Big Jock led us to great triumphs.

Tommy Kelly

CELTIC'S fantastic European Cup win in Lisbon 25 years ago remains a very special memory for me. And it also provides me with a challenge and inspiration as we attempt to bring back the glory days. I remember that the whole family gathered round the television set in our home in Dublin because it was a rare chance to see Celtic in action. It was a real occasion for people in Ireland because of their close affiliations with Celtic and excitement was tremendous as kick-off time neared. I recall the sense of disbelief everyone felt that Celtic were still trailing going into the second half, despite having completely dominated the play. We had barely seen Inter Milan, who seemed content to defend their lead. In the end, of course, the will to attack non-stop won the day and we celebrated as if Ireland had won the World Cup. There was a sense of euphoria about Dublin. I think everyone had been watching a television set somewhere. Nobody really needs to tell me just how good Jock Stein's side was, but I am convinced they could live with the best in the modern-day game. The technical ability of every member of the Lisbon side was particularly impressive and there was the ideal blend of different strengths in the team, topped off by the genius of Jimmy Johnstone. I believe Jock Stein created a complete team without a significant weakness.

Liam Brady, in the *Celtic View* souvenir tribute on the 25th anniversary of Celtic's win in Lisbon

Fergus McCann's Message to the Fans

FERGUS McCANN wasted no time in spelling out a message of hope to the supporters in the first home match since the dramatic events of March 1994 when three directors left the club and McCann and Brian

Dempsey moved in along with Dominic Keane. The Canadian-based businessman and his former director colleague were given a rapturous reception by the 36,199 fans who attended the match against Motherwell, their highest home attendance, outwith an Old Firm match, all season. His message to the fans in the match programme that day read:

'Dear Supporter
Football is a team game. For all the stars, past and present, on and off the field, a good team overrides all that.

The message from me this afternoon, from Brian Dempsey, the other new investors in the club and our strengthened board, reflects this. In other words, individual stars, heroes, backers or whatever, have to devote their attention to working together. It applies to the football team on the field, it applies to more than 100 other people in the Celtic organisation, it applies to the investor group and share-holders. And, of course, it applies to the supporters who make everything happen.

Celtic have just undergone a dramatic and difficult change. I can tell you that the directors who have remained on the board are committed to following through on achieving the high objectives we have now agreed for Celtic Football Club. This is not the time to talk about transfer money, staff changes, family feuds or share contests; this is the time to join together in a new beginning for this great institution that is Celtic.

We all have the same aim. Let's be patient, be team players and build on this new foundation. I expect to be working in this job for about five years – answerable to all of you – and, with the support of all the others and you, I am sure it will be a rewarding period.

I certainly am committed to doing all I can, but I am only one person. Many people made this change happen, and many more are needed to back the team – and the board – to take us onward and upward.

Hail, Hail the Celts are here.'

Fergus McCann, Celtic Programme, 26 March 1994

John Thomson and Johnny Doyle – their Memories Live On

JOHN THOMSON and Johnny Doyle came from totally different backgrounds. They had little in common but one thing that united them was their love for Celtic. And both have been immortalised in verse by the fans who shared their feeling for the club.

John Thomson, the quiet, unassuming lad from Fife, died on Saturday, 5 September 1931, after a fatal collision with Sam English at Ibrox. Transferred from Ibrox to the Victoria Infirmary, he died there of a depressed fracture of the skull at 9.25 p.m. A crowd of more than 30,000 packed Bowhill Cemetery to pay tribute to the Prince of Goalkeepers. The following Saturday the fans at Parkhead stood silent and the goal lay empty before the Celtic *v* Queen's Park game. A two-minute silence was broken only by the poignant sound of the *The Last Post* – a tribute to a heroic keeper.

Countless tributes were paid to the skill and bravery of the young Fifer and J.C. in the *Glasgow Observer* wrote this glowing memorial:

> In the heart of the Shamrock he stands,
> The laddie with magical hands,
> We can never forget,
> We still think of him yet –
> Why he died only God understands.
> He was proud of Celtic's jersey to don,
> Our swift-footed, sure-handed John,
> With his slim boyish grace,
> Time can never efface,
> The memory of him who is gone.

Johnny Doyle, whose dashing wing play earned him great praise, was an extra-special favourite of the fans who stood in the Jungle. His marvellous turn of speed and extrovert character endeared him to the fans and to his team-mates, who loved his cheery style. Death came suddenly and unexpectedly for John on 19 October 1981, when he was electrocuted while working on the installation of a light-fitting in his Kilmarnock home.

Billy McNeill summed him up, saying, 'Johnny Doyle was the epitome of the phrase "a true Celt".' His popularity with the fans was shown when Celtic retained the league title in 1982 by beating St Mirren at Parkhead. Taking their cue from the fans in the Jungle, the supporters chanted, 'We've won the league for Doyle.'

Later, Mr T. Tobin, of Easterhouse, Glasgow, wrote this poem in memory of a wholehearted Celt:

> Our Man on the Field
> He was one of us,
> Bedecked in our green
> Our representative on the field
> As one with the Jungle
> And just as keen,
> Our Man on the Field.
> Ninety minutes,
> Of give and take,
> His wounds were quickly healed,
> His beloved jersey,
> He'd ne'er forsake.
>
> Our Man on the Field.
> His colour was ours,
> Emerald Green,
> To its derisors he'd never yield,
> That great supporter,
> So small and lean,
> Our Man on the Field.
> He typified us all,
> And lived our dream,
> His immortality is sealed,
> Johnny Doyle
> In the Celtic team,
> was our
> Man on the Field.

JUST thinking about this tie excites the imagination. This week's sale of 50,000 tickets by Celtic on one afternoon shows just how the tie has caught the fancy of the fans. It's more than just the clash of the countries' two top teams, of course. It is a two-legged set-to between the noisiest, most publicised, most biased fans in Britain, perhaps in Europe, possibly in the world.

It's the Parkhead Jungle versus the Anfield Kop.

The Liverpool fans who come to Parkhead certainly will do their darnedest to make themselves heard. They have a reputation to defend. A reputation born on the Kop, a lollopy, old-fashioned structure which umbrellas 20,000 leather-lunged Liverpudlians who believe, with as blind a faith as any Celtic fan, that there *is* no other team than the Reds. The Kopites swirl and sway, rock and roll. They are bawdy, blatant exhibitionists. They've got a Beatle-touch flair for improvising on the spur of the moment.

The Jungle, that corrugated-roofed iron shelter, houses 10,000 fanatical green-and-white-scarved Celtic fans whose support for their team can get through the toughest hide of the most hardened of opposition.

It's not so long ago I remember an experienced Celtic player telling me he had to stuff his ears with cotton wool to keep out the awe-inspiring noise, and he declared, 'And they are *our* fans too!'

There is, undoubtedly, an ugly side of the football fanaticism as practised by the Jungle and the Kop. But bigger than this is the fact that here is the heart of football. The exciting pulse that makes you tense with expectation, speak that little bit faster, smoke that little bit more often – even before a team takes the field.

Weekly News, April 1966, just before Celtic and Liverpool met in the European Cup Winners Cup semi-final

THE atmosphere in the Jungle sometimes got a bit hairy when it was packed, but it was always good-natured. I remember being scared out of my wits at the European Cup tie with Real Madrid in 1979. Going there that night I don't think even the most optimistic Celtic fan expected us to win, but we did – 2–0 and the excitement was fantastic. At the final whistle I was being shuttled about like a pinball as everyone was hugging each other, falling about and singing at the same time. I had never seen anything like it and that was the night I realised, even at 11 years old, that the Jungle was the place for me for all time.

Gary Scott, Liverpool

IT wasn't really awkward for me to play against Celtic, in fact it sort of spurred me on. I remember scoring my first goal against them – Peter Latchford was in goal.

Anyway, a few weeks later I was in the Jungle cheering them

on as Aberdeen's game was cancelled. I was getting a few funny looks at the time.

Joe Miller, *Once a Tim*, issue 16

MY only dream was to play football for Celtic, to run out the tunnel once would have been great. I will always remember my first game at Parkhead, when we beat Hibs 3–2. I had done it. I always wanted to run out at Parkhead and run to the Jungle, if only the once. Luckily enough, I have run out to the Jungle hundreds of times since then. To lead Celtic out as skipper must be the highest accolade I could possible achieve as a Celtic player.

Peter Grant, *Once a Tim*, on being asked how it felt to be made captain of Celtic and lead the team out the tunnel

I WAS at the 'boycott' game against Kilmarnock in March 1994 when a fox ran across the park and, quick as a flash, a punter in the crowd said: 'We've got Basil Fawlty on the Board and Basil Brush on the park.'

Tommy Kelly, Blantyre

MY earliest memory of watching Celtic was the 1967 European Cup final. When Stevie Chalmers scored, my dad and big brother Tommy danced around the living-room and fell on top of me. It's the earliest memory I have of anything. The most memorable game was the 4–2 win over Rangers in 1979. I was in the Jungle right in line with Murdo MacLeod when he scored the fourth goal.

Pat Nevin, *Once a Tim*, October 1991

Chapter Fourteen

Pass the Humble Pie

THE concluding chapter of this exercise in nostalgia, first time around, contained probably the most prophetic words ever uttered by former Celtic director Tom Grant.

That was four years ago – but they are surely worthy of repetition. In answer to a question, posed by me, about the future of the stadium, Tom made an unequivocal statement saying: 'Celtic Park *will* become one of the finest all-seated football stadia in Europe.'

He was quick to add, however, that the memory of the Jungle will live on forever.

At that time, in 1994, Grant, who held the position of the Stadium Manager, was having lengthy discussions with builders, architects and other interested parties associated with the rebuilding and total refurbishing of Celtic Park.

Said Tom: 'I say *will* and not *may* when we're talking of the ambitious redevelopment scheme,' adding that he could assure the Celtic supporters they were going to get the very best that modern technology and building could devise after intensive studies of the finest stadia – not only in Britain but in Europe. He continued: 'When completed it will be the finest in the land and one of which even the most critical fan will be immensely proud.' *He never spoke a truer word!*

Right here and now, however, I am sure there are many around the country who will have to say 'pass the humble pie' – and I count myself among their number – for I, and very many more, were sceptical that such a transformation would take place. For my lack of faith I am happy to hold up my hands and accept my penance. I admit my scepticism was unfounded and I am delighted to heartily applaud Fergus McCann for his magnificent achievement in providing arguably one of the finest football stadia in Europe.

The fourth anniversary of that historic take-over at Celtic, when fan-power altered for all time the course of the history of a great football club, was celebrated on 4 March 1998. From being only seven minutes away from total wipe-out, this club is now one of the most prosperous football organisations in Europe. In that darkest hour, four years ago, there were just 140 shareholders controlling the destiny of Celtic. Within a year of Fergus McCann's revolution more than 10,000 supporters had pledged themselves, and their cash, to the club in an unmitigated display of loyalty and devotion.

It was an unprecedented move in British football and the most successful football share issue of its time. Shares started out at £64 but soared to a high of £350 as McCann's dream came true. Attendances also rocketed in keeping with the club's changing status and, as Fergus entered the fifth and final year of his tenure here, the capacity of the stadium rose to 60,000 – making it the biggest club stadium in Britain.

Tom Grant's words were certainly truly prophetic. Before McCann and Brian Dempsey made their historic announcement that 'the rebels have won', those in power at Celtic had been satisfied with a 7,100 strong list of season book holders. That figure was dwarfed as the 7,000 grew to more than 40,000 with an astonishing waiting list of some 10,000 patiently standing by for the completion of the new West Stand (to be named after Jock Stein). With gates averaging around 48,000 plus, there was also a phenomenal increase in the sale of Celtic's retail goods.

An income of £424,000 was reported in June of 1994 and it's a safe bet that the bulk of that will have come after the take-over in March of that year.

Incredibly, up to January of 1998 – just less than four years after the coup – an astonishing £2.1 million had been taken, and this was on the increase with every passing week. To cope with this fantastic demand Celtic launched a new Superstore at the park, and such is the success of this venture that the commercial department were soon dealing with almost 3,500 customers on matchdays. Catering facilities have been an integral part of the success story with the opening of the North Stand, on the site of the Jungle, bringing another five large and spacious lounges as well as the prestigious Captain's Table restaurant being called into play. The days of the old standby of pie and Bovril have been supplemented by pizza, pakora and the like, and while partaking of these delicacies you can watch matches on television on one of the many monitors throughout the stadium.

But Celtic have not forgotten their roots and within the last few months the club has allocated more than £100,000 to charities and is involved in work in the local community much more than ever before. On-field commitments will always, of course, be paramount to this club and the departure of the management team of Tommy Burns and Bill Stark saw the arrival of Celtic's first ever foreign coach – Wim Jansen. The Dutchman linked up quickly and successfully with former Celtic stalwart Murdo MacLeod, with the appointment of Jock Brown as Football General Manager allowing Wim and Murdo to get on with their coaching jobs.

At the time of writing, Fergus McCann was maintaining he would adhere to his promise that he would retire after five years with the club.

There can be no denying that he has made a magnificent contribution to the history of the club and, if nothing else, he has left an incredible legacy to the supporters in the shape of the new stadium and the rock solid infrastructure of the club. Fergus is not the type of man to gloat, but he must have achieved great satisfaction at the growth of the club during his time in office. He said: 'These are exciting times for Celtic Park. Everyone is working very hard in their aim to ensure that the dreams of our supporters are realised.'

He added: 'I know that many people doubted our plans for a 60,000 all-seated stadium and felt it would be some kind of white elephant. However these voices are silent now as the Celtic support has driven the club forward . . . whether it be share issue, season tickets, merchandise or backing the team home and away. Celtic have committed £2 million plus, over the period, on new players and around £30 million on building the stadium.'

CHAPTER FIFTEEN

How the Old Place has Changed

IAN PAUL, *The Herald*'s award-winning sports journalist, is a veteran of the press boxes of Europe – a man whose skill with the pen, the laptop and the phone has taken him to the finest sporting stadia in pursuit of articles on, among other items, football, racing, golf and boxing.

One of his finest hours, and most certainly his saddest, was his excellent coverage of the Heysel Disaster, which was one of the main reasons for the change in Britain's soccer stadia.

Ian has been covering football since long before the days of all-seated stadia and can readily recall Celtic Park in the days of the Jungle, and Ibrox with its high and packed terracings. Here, however, he writes of a recent encounter with a Celtic supporter with mixed feelings of pride in the new stadium and longing for the days of yesteryear.

THE MAN wore a camel-hair coat that clearly cost a great deal more than his season ticket, gold jangled on his wrists and the tanned face indicated a less demanding winter sojourn elsewhere. It was that appearance which made the words he spoke all the more incongruous. He was in the main stand at Celtic Park, whiling away the minutes before the kick-off, when he pointed across to the imposing new North Stand, with its arms cuddling each end of the pitch like a protective mother: 'You won't believe this,' he said, 'but part of me longs for the old Jungle'.

At first it seemed such a ludicrous statement, and I suppose he realised it himself, but when he expanded his thoughts it became at least comprehensible: 'That is the finest stand we'll ever see in Britain, let alone Scotland,' he said, 'and this stadium is going to be the best in the UK. I am proud to be part of it. I am also proud to be able to follow the tradition in my family and support my team. What slightly bothers me is that I wonder if we have the same togetherness and sense of comradeship that my dad and his friends had when they stood over there in the Jungle.' He could recall being lofted over the turnstiles by his father and being hoisted on to the wall at the back of the terracing. 'I have very fond memories of those days and the great banter that went on below me as the men cracked jokes and cheered the great names on the day.'

Perhaps that is the paradox of progress; that the wonderful new Parkhead, which had to be conceived and achieved if the club was to be a force going into the next century, inevitably would also draw the final curtain on an age when cloth caps proliferated and the people's game really did belong to the people. When the old Jungle area was razed to the ground and building began back in November 1994, on the stand that was to hold 26,000 people, there would be many older Celtic fans who would feel the same way as that gentleman in the expensive coat. Yet, as each new girder hoisted its fingers high into the sky, creating a startling, modernistic, multi-million pound vista overlooking one of the poorest areas in Glasgow, it was hard for them, as with others from every part of town and beyond, not to feel a thrill at being present at a new beginning. Nor was it necessary to be a card-carrying Celtic supporter either to appreciate that this immense tangle of steel, which grew stage by stage into the viewing arena that generates the most intimidating and exciting noise in the sport in this country, was something extraordinary.

Of course, it is also easy to believe, along with the descendants of former Jungle regulars, that the ghosts of great players, great names of the century still flit across the turf in front of this vast all-seated complex. They left their mark on generations and the generations that followed, so why would it be unusual for them to return and experience the joy of doing their thing in front of the gang of the nineties? If you are unable to see the waif-like Patsy Gallacher wriggling his way into the penalty area, Jimmy McGrory bulleting in a header from 20 yards, Charlie Tully having a seat on the ball, or

Jimmy Johnstone corkscrewing defenders into the grass, then perhaps your imagination is in need of therapy.

Those players and a host of others who entertained, thrilled and enthralled football fans through the century are as much a part of the new Parkhead as the cement and girders. Even so, this miracle of modern construction was seen at its finest when the grand replacement for the Jungle was opened in 1995. It represented space-age ingenuity and viewing facilities of the highest quality. There can be no argument with any of that, but it remains the case that no technology in the world can destroy memory banks . . . just ask the man in the camel-hair coat.

Ian Paul

Joe Has Seen It, Done It All – from Wearing the Scarf to the Wedding Suit!

JOE SULLIVAN spent his formative years on the gentle slopes of the Jungle. From being a supporter he graduated into journalism, as a reporter, and finally to editing the *Celtic View*. But, his love affair with the Hoops extended beyond that . . . he even held his wedding reception on the site of what had once been his old stomping ground of the Jungle! He still suffers pangs of regret at the passing of his old haunts but willingly sacrifices his feelings in favour of progress back to dominance. Here are his feelings, graphically spelt out, as he bears witness to the culmination of a dream at finally seeing the rise of a great stadium.

WHEN this book first hit the streets, in 1994, the vast majority of Celtic supporters simply didn't know what to expect. We realised that the Jungle, along with the two goal ends of the stadium, was being demolished. But what precisely was in store for us all was a mystery – and there were some of us who feared the worst. The Jungle had been the cornerstone of Celtic Park for decades and the vibrancy of a support, revered the world over, was generated by the throng that congregated in that relatively small area.

The mind and memory play tricks and I expect many of us recall the *immense* stretch of concrete interspersed with metal barriers. In truth, it was roughly 100 yards by 20 yards and was dwarfed even then by the expanses of the Celtic and Rangers ends. Though, like Jungle favourite Jimmy Johnstone, the heart beating within was bigger than the body housing it. And now, the ghost of the building that was the Jungle is dwarfed even further by the huge colossus that rose, like the phoenix from the ashes, in the months following the demolition.

Four years after the initial publication of *Jungle Tales* we can rest assured that those apprehensions of '94 were unfounded. Hindsight is an amazing tool, and one which can also bend the memory banks, but how many of us recall that when the bulldozers moved in, planning permission for the new structure wasn't even in place. A massive gamble you may think, but such was Fergus McCann's belief and determination to completely rebuild Celtic Park (and remember those who had their eyes turned towards Cambuslang said it couldn't be done), and now the reality is there – staring us in the face at every home game.

The amazing transformation may now be taken for granted, but harking back to the dark days of the early nineties it is still frightening to think on what could have been.

However, Celtic Park is now the finest stadium in the country, and the area straddled by the Jungle now seats 26,000, in comparison to standing to standing 10,000 tops when it was bursting at the seams. And from now on over 60,000 can be seated within Celtic Park with season books at a premium – over 50,000 in total. Who would have thought that when Fergus McCann announced he was looking for the 10,000 missing Celtic supporters, his own estimation would be magnified to such a great extent?

We are proud of this stadium, but it is the pride that still burns for the Jungle that inspired this book. Just think about it. This is not a history of the club, it is not about one of the legendary Celts from days of yore – it is not even about the stadium. It is about a patch of concrete covered by a not too practical or weather-proof stretch of corrugated material that never exactly made it into any brochures featuring the local beauty spots. But how many clubs could claim such a distinction – to have a book written about just one part of the ground, never mind have the book go into reprint? I'm honoured to be writing this article for John's book in my position as editor of the *Celtic View*.

And that, in itself, throws up an irony, for in the days before I was employed by the club I had only ever been in the South Stand on *two* occasions. The first was in the late seventies when my 'fixed odds' coupon came up and I reneged on the Jungle to treat myself to a seat in the stand for a midweek game against Motherwell – I wasn't in too much of a hurry to get back.

The second time I had a seat in the stand was when I took my then 14-month-old son Niall to his first Celtic game. His next match was a couple of years later and he was a toddler – running about at the back of the Jungle. It was the part of the ground that meant most to the majority of the support and I was proud to take my place there whenever Celtic were at home. So much so that looking at old photographs of the Jungle is akin to leafing through pictures of family members now gone.

However, times move on and Celtic approach the millennium with a stadium we are honoured to take our seats in. Even more than seats! I tied the knot on 10 October 1997 and the wedding reception was held in the lounges of the north stand – if you had told me that I would go through all that on what is basically the Jungle roof, then I simply wouldn't have believed you! That is a measure of how Celtic and football have changed since the days of pies, Bovril, standing in pouring rain and other such Scottish traditions. But we still have cherished memories and can look back with pride at the dilapidated structure that maybe only *we* appreciated.

I was brought up in Possil's Stony Hurst and, while I may not want to live there now (like the Jungle it has been demolished), I still love being there and the same can be said of the old north terracing. We may have given up a great many things when the bulldozers moved in, but:

> If losing the Jungle meant building a stadium of dreams – then it was worth it.
>
> If losing the jungle meant over 50,000 season book holders – then it was worth it.
>
> If losing the Jungle meant attracting quality players to break the Ibrox stranglehold on the championship – then it was worth it!
>
> **Joe Sullivan**

'Jungle Ghosts' with a Smile on their Faces

CELTIC supporters' affection for the world-renowned Jungle will never diminish – with the old standing area having been adopted as an integral part of the folklore of an institution. But even for those who had spent their boyhoods in the Jungle, the sight of the magnificent new structure on the spot where the Jungle stood is awesome. When filled to capacity, as it on every matchday, it is assuredly one of the most glorious sights on the European football stage.

This was never more clearly illustrated than on the last league day of the 1997–98 season when Celtic, under the inspirational leadership of captain Tom Boyd and the masterminded by head coach Wim Jansen ably assisted by Murdo MacLeod, finally broke Rangers' stranglehold on the league championship. Unfortunately for the Celtic supporters their euphoria was dealt a swift and savage blow when Jansen, the first foreign coach to achieve such success in Scotland, resigned citing an inability to work with general manager Jock Brown.

The Hoops had gone into this crucial 90 minutes knowing victory was essential if Rangers' domination was to be brought to an end as Walter Smith's men sought to surpass Celtic's marvellous achievement of winning nine titles in a row. Boyd's Bhoys did it – beating St Johnstone 2–0 with goals by Swede Henrik Larsson and Norwegian Harald Brattbakk – while Rangers saw their hopes dashed, despite beating Dundee United 2–1. The scenes of jubilation were something to behold! Not even a jam-packed Jungle, crammed with scarf-waving fans, could have bettered this sight of sights. Well . . . maybe! But, I am certain the ghosts of the countless thousands of Celtic fans who had stood on very many occasions over previous decades, would have been proud of the reception their successors gave their heroes as yet another piece of Celtic history was written into the tablets of stone for generations of fans to revere in years to come. The incredible scenes of rejoicing, which started before a ball was kicked with a magnificent rendition of

'You'll Never Walk Alone' with 50,000 voices in unison, was something which made the short hairs stand on the necks of those privileged to be there to savour this unforgettable occasion.

Then at the finish the fans went into party mode, both at the park and in almost every corner of the city and surrounding area. Players such as Larsson, Brattbakk, Reiper and Stubbs declared later they had never witnessed such scenes of rejoicing. The resignation of Jansen, even although it was not a major surprise after weeks of talk of rifts between the head coach and the general manager, cast a huge shadow over the celebrations. But the fans have grown accustomed to self-inflicted wounds suffered in recent years, and the majority of them are certain the club will once more fight back from the adversity to consolidate its place back on top after a decade spent in the wilderness.